OZ CLAR
WINE COMPANION
CHAMPAGNE
AND ALSACE

GUIDE
DAVID COBBOLD

De Agostini Editions

HOW TO USE THIS BOOK

MAPS

For further information on the wine regions see the Fold-out Map.

Each tour in the book has a map to accompany it. These are not detailed road maps; readers are advised to buy such maps to avoid local navigation difficulties.

═══ Motorway (*Autoroute*)

▬▬ Major road

──── Minor road

──── Other road

FACT FILES

Each tour has an accompanying fact file, which lists sources of information on the region, markets and festivals, and where to buy wine. There is also a short listing of hotels and restaurants.

Ⓗ Hotel
Ⓡ Restaurant

To give an indication of prices, we have used a simple rating system.

Ⓕ Inexpensive
ⒻⒻ Moderate
ⒻⒻⒻ Expensive

WINE PRODUCERS

Producers' names in small capitals refer to entries in the A–Z on page 70.

Visiting arrangements
✔ Visitors welcome
◔ By appointment
✘ No visitors

Wine styles made
🍷 Red
🍷 White
🍷 Rosé
🍷 Sparkling

Please note that guidebook information is inevitably subject to change. We suggest that, wherever possible, you telephone in advance to check addresses, opening times, etc.

While every care has been taken in preparing this guide, the publishers cannot accept any liability for any consequence arising from the use of information contained in it.

First published
by De Agostini Editions
Griffin House
161 Hammersmith Road
London W6 8SD

Distributed in the U.S.
by Stewart, Tabori & Chang,
a division of US Media
Holdings Inc
115 West 18th Street, 5th Floor
New York NY10011

Distributed in Canada
by General Publishing
Company Ltd
30 Lesmill Road, Don Mills
Ontario M3B 2T6

Oz Clarke's Wine Companion:
Champagne and Alsace
copyright © 1997 Websters
International Publishers

Fold-out Map
copyright © 1997 Websters
International Publishers
Text copyright © 1997
Oz Clarke
Maps copyright © 1997
Websters International Publishers
Some maps and text have been
adapted from *Oz Clarke's Wine
Atlas* copyright © 1995 Websters
International Publishers

Guide
copyright © 1997 Websters
International Publishers

Created and designed by Websters
International Publishers Ltd
Axe & Bottle Court
70 Newcomen Street
London SE1 1YT

UK ISBN: 1 86212 049 8
A CIP catalogue record for this book is available from the British Library.

US ISBN: 1 86212 047 1
Library of Congress Catalog
Card Number 97–66612

OZ CLARKE

Oz Clarke is one of the world's leading wine experts, with a formidable reputation based on his extensive wine knowledge and accessible, no-nonsense approach. He appears regularly on BBC Television and has won all the major wine-writing awards in the USA and UK. His bestselling titles include *Oz Clarke's Wine Atlas*, *Oz Clarke's Pocket Wine Guide* and the *Microsoft Wine Guide* CD-ROM.

DAVID COBBOLD

David Cobbold has lived and worked in France for over 20 years, mainly in the wine trade. He is now a wine consultant, working worldwide. He also writes on wine for both British and French publications. This is his third book.

Associate Editorial Director
Fiona Holman
Associate Art Director
Nigel O'Gorman
Art Editor
Christopher Howson
Sub-editor
Gwen Rigby
Editorial Assistant
Emma Richards
Wine Consultant
Phillip Williamson
DTP
Jonathan Harley
Production
Kâren Smith
Index
Naomi Good
Editorial Director
Claire Harcup
Pictorial Cartography
Keith and Sue Gage,
Contour Designs
Pictorial Map Editor
Wink Lorch
Touring Maps
European Map Graphics

Colour separations by Columbia
Offset, Singapore
Printed in Hong Kong

Photographs:
Front cover The medieval village of Riquewihr is one of Alsace's main wine centres.
Page 1 The Alsace wine route meanders along the eastern foothills of the Vosges.
Page 3 Gewurztraminer reaches its peak in Alsace.

Contents

Visiting the cellars of a great Champagne house, here Louis Roederer in Reims, and seeing the intricate procedures at first hand is one of the main tourist attractions of the region.

Introduction

Little more than an hour to the north-east of Paris are the valleys of Champagne, the area that gives its name to the world's greatest sparkling wine. Only three hours' drive further east, woven into the wooded slopes of the Vosges mountains, is Alsace, with wines unlike any others in France. These are two of France's greatest vineyard regions.

The sheer difference between the wine styles – Champagne foaming and celebratory; Alsace perfumed, exotic and heady – seems at first to be matched by the landscape and the towns. Wine activity in Champagne seems centred on the towns – Reims, Épernay, Ay – and there is an impressive but standoffish *hauteur* about the various companies' headquarters. In Alsace, the heart of the wine world seems to beat in the bustling, little villages that cling to the hillsides below the deep, dark forests of the Vosges. In Champagne you are always aware that this is basically a cold region, although the geological quirks that threw up the limestone slopes to the north and south of the Marne offer

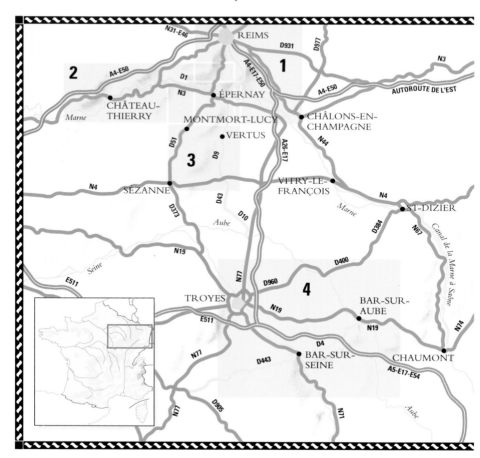

temporary respite, so long as the sun is shining on you. In Alsace, as you luxuriate in the warm dry days you feel as though you're cocooned in a vineyard shangri-la.

But there are similarities too. As you stand on the Montagne de Reims and look out on the plains to the northeast, remind yourself that you are positioned on the last natural defence before Paris. For centuries these plains have seen brutal warfare and the scars of the last two World Wars lie only just below the surface. Now let's stand in the great Sporen vineyard just beneath Riquewihr, a fairytale jumble of houses scarcely changed since medieval times. And look out toward the mighty river Rhine. Here, you're standing on France's natural eastern frontier and every great struggle between Germany and France has seen these lovely hills battered by cannon fire. Yet through such adversity, both regions have forged a personality as individual as any in France. And in Champagne, away from the main towns you will find villages as full of bustle as any in Alsace, with numerous growers inviting you in to taste and buy their wines.

Oz Clarke

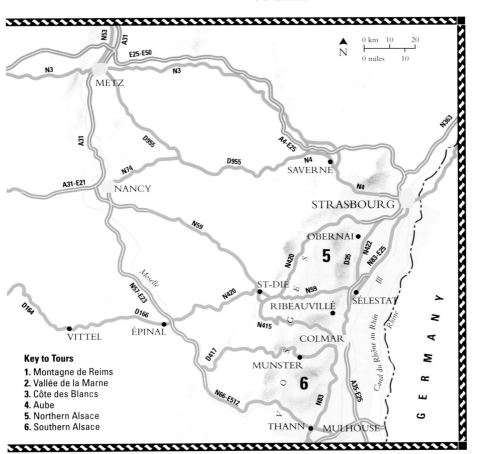

Key to Tours
1. Montagne de Reims
2. Vallée de la Marne
3. Côte des Blancs
4. Aube
5. Northern Alsace
6. Southern Alsace

Champagne at a Glance

'La Champagne' in northern France is the only place in the world real Champagne can come from and it is now illegal to use the term 'Champagne' or 'méthode champenoise' outside the region. As sparkling wine grows in popularity worldwide, Champagne is becoming an ever-smaller percentage of global production (currently well under 10 per cent), but it continues to be prized for its elegance, finesse and ability to age.

Typical non-vintage Champagne, such as Mercier Brut (left) is pale, despite being made from black grapes. Pommery Rosé is one of the few that gains its pink colour by contact with black grape skins (most are made by adding a little red wine).

Grape Varieties

Three grape varieties are now planted in Champagne to the exclusion of everything else and are well suited to its chalky subsoils. Pinot Noir and Chardonnay have become synonymous not only with Champagne but with the finest quality sparkling wines from anywhere in the world.

Pinot Noir

The famous grape of Burgundy covers just over one-third of the vineyard area of Champagne – the most renowned sites include the Grand Cru vineyards of the Montagne de Reims. It brings body, structure, depth and finesse to a

Pinot Noir

blend. While it lacks the colour and intensity of fruit found further south in Burgundy, these are not required in the pale, delicate wines of Champagne. It is also responsible for the rare still red wines of the region, such as Bouzy Rouge, light but perfumed with raspberry fruit.

Chardonnay

The vines of the world's most popular grape variety become tough and vigorous in the harsh northern climate of Champagne, and a susceptibility to spring frosts can

Chardonnay

impair both yield and quality. Chardonnay brings a honeyed, floral component to blends, and develops good fruit richness with age. Blanc de Blancs Champagne is made from 100 per cent Chardonnay.

Pinot Meunier

Softer, fruitier, more perfumed than both Chardonnay and Pinot Noir, Pinot Meunier has less aging potential but gives richness to youthful wines. It makes up more than a third of the blend in much non-vintage Champagne.

Pinot Meunier

CLASSIFICATIONS

Champagne AC One regional appellation covers all the sparkling wines of the region, regardless of style. The wine can be blended from all three grape varieties or, more rarely, made from a single variety. Blanc de Blancs is from Chardonnay and Blanc de Noirs from Pinot Noir.

There is, in addition, an *échelle des crus*, or 'ladder of growths', in which villages are classified according to the quality of their vineyards, on a scale ranging from 100 per cent for the finest villages down to 80 per cent.

Grand Cru This category comprises 17 villages which are rated 100 per cent and receive that percentage of the agreed price for grapes at harvest time. Those growers with sought-after vineyards negotiate a premium to ensure their loyalty to a particular Champagne house.

Premier Cru This is a large category of 41 villages which are rated at between 99 and 90 per cent.

Other villages The remaining wine villages, of which there are more than 200, are rated at between 89 and 80 per cent.

Coteaux Champenois AC Red, white and rosé still wines. A village name may be stated on the label, e.g. Bouzy Rouge.

Rosé des Riceys AC Deep-coloured rosé made from Pinot Noir only in the ripest years in the village of les Riceys in the southern Aube.

Understanding Champagne

You can learn something about a wine simply by looking at the bottle. Here, the standard bottle shape and design have been replaced by more decorative packaging.

The standard bottle used for most non-vintage Champagne is similar to the Burgundy bottle, with low sloping shoulders, but with a heavy lip for securing the wire muzzle.

Lavish use of gold foil has long been part of the design concept behind the marketing of Champagne to project a prestige image.

A heavier bottle than normal is needed to withstand 5–6 atmospheres of pressure; dark glass offers the Champagne inside optimum protection from light and heat.

Brut indicates a dry or almost dry style of Champagne.

Champagne is the only AC not required to have the words *appellation contrôlée* on the label.

Veuve Clicquot's Brut non-vintage Champagne has a distinctive, light orange label with finely scrolled lettering.

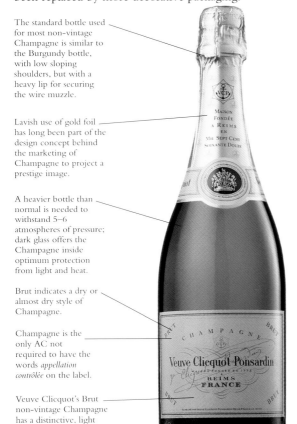

VINTAGES

Most Champagne is made as a non-vintage wine. It should be at its best, or near it, when released, although some can improve further with a little age. Vintage Champagne, made only in the best years, is held back for longer before release (usually about 6 years from the harvest). Depending on the house style and the nature of the vintage, bottles may then be cellared for 10 years or more.

1996 A dry summer produced a very high-quality harvest.
1995 Shows good potential with careful selection, given some high-quality fruit.
1991 A number of vintage wines were produced, but not much is exciting.
1990 The best of a trio of fine vintages, rich and structured.
1989 Lush, showy wines, often low in acidity. Many are ready now, although the really top names can still improve.
1988 Firm, even steely wines that are refined and ageworthy.
1986 Choose with care – much of the wine was more suited to blending.
1985 Firm fine wines; small quantities from the best producers continue to improve.
1982 Rich, powerful wines, low in acidity, that continue to develop. Many are drinking well now.
1981 A small crop, but the few wines made are mostly still good.
Older vintages 1979s are balanced; 1976 was a year of ripe bold wines that seemed likely to be outshone by the refined harmonious 1975s, but this has not always been the case; 1973 favoured elegance.
Other good years 1971 70 69 66 64 62 61 52 49 47 45.

GLOSSARY

Base wine Still wine prior to SECOND FERMENTATION.
Blanc de Blancs Champagne made only from Chardonnay.
Blanc de Noirs Champagne made only from black grapes.
Brut Dry or almost so, with a residual sugar level of less than 15g per litre. If less than 6g, the wine may be labelled Extra Brut. Brut Zéro or Brut Nature indicates none at all.
Champagne method This includes a SECOND FERMENTATION in the bottle.
Coopérative Manipulant (CM) Champagne co-operative.
Cuvée Prestige A house's most expensive bottling, which should be, though is not always, its best.
Dosage Sugar and wine solution added before the final bottling, which determines the sweetness of the Champagne.

Doux Sweet.
Fermentation (alcoholic) Conversion of grape sugar into alcohol and carbon dioxide with the aid of yeasts.
Grande Marque Member of the 'Syndicat des Grandes Marques', a long-standing association of the most prestigious large Champagne houses.
Marque d'Acheteur (MA) Buyer's own brand or label.
Millésime French for vintage.
Négociant-Manipulant (NM) Champagne house which makes and sells Champagne from some or all bought-in grapes.
Non-vintage Champagne based in theory on a blend from several years, but usually based on the last year, and sold without a vintage date.
Récoltant-Manipulant (RM) A grower who makes and sells Champagne from his own grapes.
Remuage/Riddling Art of moving

the lees down into the neck of the bottle prior to *dégorgement*. Traditionally done by hand but increasingly carried out in automated gyropalettes.
Reserve wine Wine from older vintages held in reserve to make up blends with younger wine for non-vintage Champagne.
Rosé Pink wine; the law allows it to be made by blending a little red wine with white, although some makers adhere to the usual method of keeping the black grape skins in contact with the juice for a period.
Sec, Demi-Sec Sweeter styles of Champagne with residual sugar levels of 17–35g and 33–50g per litre.
Second Fermentation Small second alcoholic fermentation which gives Champagne its sparkle.
Vintage Champagne of a single, usually superior, year.

Brilliant but pale Cave de Turckheim Pinot Noir (left) is made from the only permitted red grape, which accounts for less than 10 per cent of Alsace wine. The golden Vendange Tardive Domaines Schlumberger Gewurztraminer deepens with age.

Alsace at a Glance

Although Alsace owes much to Germany in terms of history, the growth and revival of its largely family-owned wine estates in the 20th century have taken place under French laws. Primary grape flavours and aromas are given great emphasis, reflected in the fact that Alsace is the only French AC to state the grape variety on the label. Despite its heritage, there is also a particular dryness, a fruit quality and a fragance that owes nothing to either country – a style that is distinctly Alsace.

Grape Varieties

White grapes predominate in Alsace and three in particular – Gewurztraminer, Riesling and Pinot Gris – stand out, either as varietals or individual blended wines. They make up less than half the total plantings but account for most of the premium styles. Pinot Noir is the only red grape variety.

Gewurztraminer

Alsace wines are renowned for their flowery spice and most distinctive are the strong, spicy, intense flavours of Gewurztraminer. Gewürz means spice in German and these are typically big, fat, spicy wines with overt grapy, sometimes lychee, flavours, often thick with the richness of oriental fruit, but they are also capable of showing a more refined floral, perfumed and rosewater character. These flavours are most obvious in Vendange Tardive wines. Gewurztraminer wines are almost always dry and high in alcohol but with lowish acidity levels.

Gewurztraminer

Riesling

Considered to be the most classic Alsace variety, Riesling here produces great, long-lived, dry wines that are powerful, structured and steely and grow 'petrolly' with age. It also makes excellent late-harvest sweet wines. Compared to German Rieslings, Alsace ones have a higher

Riesling

alcohol level but the acidity is lower, and they are often drier and fuller. Vibrant peach and citrus flavours intensify with age and an oily, spicy, earthy or petrolly character becomes accentuated. The subtleties of Grand Cru soils are most evident with Riesling, a late-ripening variety.

Pinot Gris

Pinot Gris grapes can be anything between greyish blue and brownish pink and in the vineyard the variety is often mistaken for Pinot Noir. Pinot Gris used to be called Tokay d'Alsace and many wines are still labelled Tokay-Pinot Gris. They

Pinot Gris

tend to have relatively high alcohol and acidity levels but are a little fatter than most other Alsace whites. Like nearly all Alsace whites they are almost always made dry. A deep-coloured, golden wine, the flavours can be rich, honeyed and nutty and even the lighter wines are luscious behind their dry fruit. The best ones can age well.

Other Varieties

Muscat is the fourth so-called 'noble' variety of Alsace, but the wine is shorter-lived and not so readily fashioned into the richer, sweeter styles. Relatively low in alcohol and acidity, it is normally made into a bone-dry wine with a fragrant taste of freshly picked grapes. Pinot Blanc produces light, appley, creamy-soft wines and is the most important constituent of Crémant d'Alsace. Auxerrois is a variety allowed in the production of Pinot Blanc wine, but it is fuller and rounder with a distinct spicy, citrus orange character. Light, tart and slightly earthy Sylvaner used to be the basic Alsace grape, along with the unmemorable Chasselas, but Pinot Blanc has now largely taken over this job. Pinot Noir, Alsace's only red variety, suffers an image problem even though formerly pale, insipid red and rosé wines are now being replaced by richer, oakier versions.

Understanding Alsace Wine

Alsace wine labels are the most informative in France, since varietal labelling is part of the appellation laws. The full wine name includes the producer, the grape variety, the site and the style of wine.

EU regulations now require the capsule to be made of tin foil or plastic instead of lead.

The neck label emphasizes the vintage. A coat of arms is typical for a producer with a long family history.

The traditional Alsace fluted bottle is also used for the small amount of red produced, making it harder to sell.

Family ownership is very common in Alsace, be it a relatively large producer such as Domaines Schlumberger, or one of more than 3000 small growers represented by 18 co-operatives.

Kitterlé is one of the 50 Alsace Grands Crus.

Gewurztraminer is one of the four 'noble' grape varieties allowed in Grand Cru vineyards.

A punt is neither necessary nor practical for an Alsace bottle.

GLOSSARY

Acidity Important component of wine that gives it its freshness and is crucial to its balance.

Cave Co-opérative A common organization in French wine areas. It caters for the grape grower who has no means of making his own wine.

Clos French term for a vineyard that was, or still is, enclosed by a wall. Mostly used in Burgundy.

Crémant French term for up-market sparkling wine made by the more expensive Champagne method. Crémant d'Alsace is usually of reasonable quality, if not great value for money.

Edelzwicker A basic blend of everyday Alsace white wine.

Lieu-dit French for a named vineyard site and commonly used in Alsace for ones that do not have Grand Cru status.

Noble rot or **Pourriture Noble** The benevolent action of the fungus *Botrytis cinerea*, shrivelling the grape and intensifying the sugar.

Terroir Physical environment of a viticultural site, comprising elements such as the soil, elevation, orientation and climate.

Varietal Wine made from a single grape variety, or showing the characteristics of one.

VINTAGES

Most Alsace wines of good concentration and adequate acidity will benefit from 3 to 5 years' aging. Only the top wines are capable of longer aging. Grand Cru wines (or equivalent) are best with 5 to 10 years' aging or more; Vendange Tardive with 5 to 15 years or more; and Sélection de Grains Nobles with 5 to 25, even 30 years, or more.

1991–1996 Recent vintages in Alsace have been somewhat variable and none can count as being truly exceptional, although the best producers have had little difficulty in creating some wines of real quality. The wines are best assessed on an individual basis.

1990 Excellent, especially the classic dry styles and Vendange Tardive wines.

1989 Superb rich Riesling, Pinot Gris and botrytized Vendange Tardive and Sélection de Grains Nobles wines.

1988 Firm, intense wines and many will continue to improve.

1985 Wonderful wines to drink now but many of them will age for longer.

1983 One of the classic Alsace vintages with many of the special bottlings now truly outstanding but capable of further age.

1976 Glorious, almost legendary wines.

Other good years 1971 69 66 64 61 59.

CLASSIFICATIONS

Alsace AC or Vin d'Alsace This is the simple generic appellation, or AC, and is normally used in conjunction with one of 8 approved grape varieties. The wine must have a minimum natural alcohol level (8.5 per cent by volume) and be bottled in the region in the traditional, slim approved Alsace 'flûte' bottle.

Vin d'Alsace Edelzwicker AC A blended wine usually based on Pinot Blanc or Sylvaner.

Alsace Grand Cru AC This is an attempt to classify the top Alsace vineyards. Stricter regulations apply and the wines must be made entirely from one of the 'noble' varieties (Gewurztraminer, Muscat, Pinot Gris and Riesling). At present there are 50 of these Grand Cru sites, mostly in the southern Haut-Rhin department.

Vendange Tardive Wine made from sweet, late-picked, almost over-ripe grapes, with a minimum level of ripeness. The wines may vary from almost dry to sweet but are usually rich.

Sélection de Grains Nobles This is the higher of the two 'super-ripe' legal descriptions. The grapes are very late-picked and are affected by botrytis, or noble rot (that creates the sweetness in Sauternes). The wines are often incredibly sweet and concentrated and able to age for decades.

Crémant d'Alsace AC Champagne-method sparkling wine from mainly Pinot Blanc but also Chardonnay, Pinot Gris, Pinot Noir or Riesling. The rosé must be from Pinot Noir.

Other Klevener de Heiligenstein is a village AC for wines from Savagnin Rosé. There is a tiny amount of Vins de Pays for wines outside the AC.

Regional Food

Andouillette, *a pork chitterling sausage, is one of Champagne's few regional specialities.*

T he north-eastern corner of France is characterized by extensive plains, where the main crops are cereals and root vegetables. In certain areas, rivers, hills and forests have produced additional foods such as funghi and fish. This is true of part of Champagne and all of Alsace. In both areas pork, accompanied by a range of green and root vegetables, has long been the mainstay of the diet. Game is plentiful, and some of France's most delicious rich cheeses come from these regions. What has undoubtedly helped the cuisine of both to develop is the local wines. This is particularly true in Champagne, where the wine is used in the preparation of most refined dishes.

Regional Produce

The greater Champagne area includes the Ardennes, to the east, where there are several specialities in charcuterie: Ardennes ham, pigs' trotters from Ste-Menehould and *boudin blanc* from Rethel. In the extreme south, *andouillette* from Troyes is famous. Rich cheeses are plentiful, with Langres, Chaource, Maroilles and the rare but wonderful Soumintrin, all from the Aube region around Troyes. In the far west, there is Brie, although its homeland overlaps into the Île de France. The wealth of Reims meant that spices found their way to the city from the Middle Ages onward, and gingerbread and other exotic forms of cake and biscuits became local specialities. Almost the only trace of this today are the *biscuits de Reims*.

The location of Alsace on the German border, and the fact that it has, at several times in the recent past, been governed by Germany, shows in the local dialect, and most dishes have Germanic names. The use of herbs and spices to heighten the flavour of meats, jams and pastries is a heritage from Central Europe. Pork was the favourite meat in Alsace until the 19th century, and it is still important. All types of sausage and ham are to be found, smoked, cured or salted, often with spices added, and there are more than 40 different varieties of pâté. Alsace is also a major producer of *pâté de foie gras*. Game is plentiful and wild boar, deer and feathered game are on most menus during autumn and winter. The Rhine and its tributaries provide fish, and although many fish have disappeared as a result of pollution and the draining of lakes, carp is a speciality of the Sundgau region south of Mulhouse.

Vegetables are plentiful, and the asparagus grown in the rich soil of the valleys is renowned for its flavour. *Choucroute*, pickled cabbage, is probably Alsace's best-known speciality. The curing of cabbage was introduced in the Middle Ages,

WINE AND FOOD IN CHAMPAGNE

A glass of Champagne precedes any meal worth its name. The lighter, crisper Blanc de Blancs is often served, but a classic Brut non-vintage, usually blended from black and white grapes, is also good. The same wines, or a rosé Champagne, go very well with terrines, pâtés and other forms of charcuterie.

Local river fish is often prepared as a form of stew known as *matelote*, which can include eel, bream, pike or carp. This is usually cooked in Champagne, and the answer is to drink the same wine as is used in the sauce. With game or red meat, try a vintage Champagne or a vintage rosé. These wines can have surprising depth and strength, and complement richer food. The alternative is the local red wine, Coteaux Champenois. This and a rosé Champagne are also excellent with cheese. Try a sweeter demi-sec Champagne with dessert – a Brut Champagne will taste unpleasantly harsh with anything sweet.

Champagne is not an area rich in local dishes, but two well-known specialities are *boudin blanc* (white sausage made from rabbit) from Rethel and *andouillette*, pork chitterling sausage, from Troyes.

An interesting speciality is Cendré, a cheese produced at the time of the grape harvest. Wood ash, dusted onto the rind to keep away the flies, is brushed off before the cheese is eaten.

Alsace food is rich and plentiful and there are many regional specialities.

In spring and early summer the local white asparagus is often served as a starter. A notorious wine killer, it can, however, be matched by the local Muscat. *Foie gras* will be complemented by the blend of sweetness and acidity in a late-harvest Riesling, Pinot Gris or Gewurztraminer. Simple *winstub* food, such as *flammeküche* or *tarte à l'oignon*, is best accompanied by Sylvaner or Pinot Blanc.

Choucroute will often have been cooked in white wine and it is well matched with a good-quality Riesling, if possible a Grand Cru, which will have the structure to stand up to the cabbage. *Baeckoffe*, which includes pork, mutton, beef, onions, potatoes, herbs, spices and white wine, also calls for a powerful Grand Cru Riesling or Pinot Gris, or a Pinot Noir, Alsace's red wine.

Munster cheese is well matched by a late-harvest Gewurztraminer, which you can then linger over during dessert.

One of the best-known dishes in Alsace is *presskopf*, in which the pig's head is turned into brawn in aspic. To prepare cabbage for *choucroute*, the heart is finely sliced and placed in a wooden barrel, where it is salted and bay leaves and juniper berries added. Layers of cabbage are alternated with salt until the barrel is full. The *choucroute* will be ready after two or three weeks of fermentation, and then it simply needs rinsing before cooking. A variation is *choucroute à l'alsacienne*, made with the addition of potatoes and several different meats, including smoked pork, sausages and bacon.

Succulent *baeckoffe* includes pork, mutton, beef, onions and potatoes, herbs, spices and white wine. It is sealed in a pastry crust and cooked slowly for several hours.

Munster is one of those cheeses whose bark is worse than its bite. Its powerful smell belies its gentle creamy texture and subtle flavours. Sometimes the crust is spiced with cumin seeds.

Desserts cover the wide variety of Alsace's fruit production – particularly in the form of fruit tarts – and the art of pastry-making.

*Lebküchle, bredl*e, *bretzel* (all types of sweet bread) are common, but *kougelhopf* – full of almonds, raisins, sugar and eggs, baked in a special fluted mould and dusted with icing sugar – is the most traditional of the rich cakes of Alsace.

and before the existence of deep-freezing it was an excellent way to conserve green vegetables for the winter. Orchards flourish in Alsace. The fruit is used in a huge range of tarts and jams and it is also distilled into many renowned *eaux de vie*, which are used in cooking and drunk as an apéritif. Pastry-making is yet another source of pride. Cheeses come mainly from the rich pastures of the Vosges mountains, the most common being Munster, from the town near Colmar.

Eating Out

It is difficult to find good country restaurants in Champagne, although there are a few excellent, and expensive, ones in relatively isolated places catering mainly to the Champagne houses and their guests. But Épernay, Troyes and Reims have a good selection, and there is a wonderful 3-star restaurant, les Crayères, on the outskirts of Reims. What makes eating out in Champagne such fun is the fact that most restaurants have a long list of excellent wines and the local brew is usually available by the glass at a reasonable price.

The wealth and diversity of local produce, linked to healthy economic conditions, have produced a plethora of restaurants of all types in Alsace. The dual culture of wine and beer (Alsace produces more than 50 per cent of France's beer) is reflected in the abundance of cosy and inexpensive *winstube* and *bierstube*, where the food is usually simple and traditional, and local wine is served by the glass or the jug. Most restaurants are family-owned and these are generally the best places for sampling local specialities. Alsace prides itself on having more restaurants with Michelin stars than any other part of France. In these restaurants, local traditions have been followed, and sometimes refined, to produce one of France's most inventive cuisines.

Villedommange's large church is a distinctive landmark along the Petite Montagne, the area of the Montagne de Reims south-west of the city.

SUMMARY OF TOURS

Montagne de Reims This top-quality Champagne area is easily explored from Reims, where hotels are plentiful. In one day this trip can provide a good overview of the landscape and the people who make Champagne. The tour visits some of Champagne's best-known wine villages, and ends in Épernay.

Vallée de la Marne Running west from Épernay toward Paris, with an optional return leg on the other side of the river, this could be the way to start, or finish, a visit to Champagne if you are travelling via Paris.

Côte des Blancs South of Épernay, this is Champagne's most intensive vine-growing area and the tour can easily be accomplished in half a day. As its name suggests, this is an area almost exclusively planted with Chardonnay, and there are some fabulous wines for those who want to spend more time tasting.

The Aube Further south, near the region's lovely old capital, Troyes, lies one of the best-kept secrets of Champagne. The rolling countryside is laced with woods, ponds and rivers, and vineyards are just one element of the landscape. Almost Burgundian in its architecture, the Aube is a relaxed and fascinating area to explore.

Touring Champagne

The Champagne region covers a far wider area than that covered by the vineyards that have made the name 'Champagne' world famous. Extremely rural and with a low population density, it stretches from the Belgian border in the north to Burgundy in the south, and from Lorraine west to the Île de France, which surrounds Paris. Only two cities have a population of more than 100,000: Reims and Troyes. The vineyards are centred around Reims and Épernay and can be divided into three main areas: the Montagne de Reims, chiefly west and south of Reims; the Marne Valley, along the river between Châlons-en-Champagne and Château-Thierry; and the Côte des Blancs, south of Épernay. There is a lesser known area south-east of Troyes in the southern Aube, around the small towns of Bar-sur-Seine and Bar-sur-Aube.

Several *autoroutes* now cross the region, making access much easier than before to reach the Champagne vineyards and a good network of minor, but often twisting, roads links the individual wine villages. Accommodation in rural areas is scarce, with the exception of *chambres d'hôte* (bed and breakfast), but Reims, Épernay and Troyes have a good selection of hotels at all price levels.

The hilly nature of most of Champagne's vineyards makes them attractive at most times of the year and, although the days are short, winter can be a good time to visit, since the lie of the land is not smothered under vegetation and the light can be spectacular. But you may prefer the spring and summer months, particularly if you want to picnic. Harvesting usually takes place in late September. Since the picking is done by hand, the otherwise quiet villages spring to life with the influx of thousands of grape pickers, and the village streets become slippery with grape juice. Do not expect the smaller growers to welcome you with open arms at this time – they will be very busy. But the large, well-known houses in Reims and Épernay have sufficient staff to look after visitors throughout the year.

Curiously, Champagne has not maintained a strong tradition of wine fairs and festivals. This is probably due to a separation between production and sales, since more than four-fifths of the vineyards belong to growers, while two-thirds of the wine is sold by *négociants*, or Champagne houses. However, St Vincent is the patron saint of grape-growers and on the weekend nearest to 22 January there are festivities in most villages, culminating in a parade at the end of January in Épernay.

Reims

The Romans created the city they called Durocortorum, around the third century AD, and Reims' first vineyards date from this period. By medieval times, Reims had become the site of the coronation of the French kings and a thriving commercial centre, trading still wine with countries to the north.

As soon as sparkling Champagne was invented and started to conquer new markets in the early 18th century, specialized trading houses sprang up in Reims, and many of those brands still survive. The Romans extracted the local *crayère*, or chalk, for construction, but little use was found for the pits until Champagne came along. Unlike almost any other wine, Champagne is aged in bottle for up to six years and, since the racks used in the course of maturing the wine take up so much space, immense cellars are indispensable. The former chalk pits, with their stable, chilly temperatures, proved perfect places for making and storing wine.

Taittinger is just one of several Champagne houses in Reims that uses a vast underground network of chalk galleries or crayères *in which to mature and store its wine.*

Many of the internationally famous Champagne houses are based in Reims. They are well aware of the promotional value of tourism and visits to their vast cellars are usually well organized and informative. The cellars can be spectacular, particularly those located in the area known as *les crayères*, behind the St-Rémi church. Among the most impressive to visit are those of Charles Heidsieck, Ruinart, Pommery, Henriot, Taittinger and Veuve Clicquot, all of whose cellars were originally quarries for the soft chalky stone that was used to build the original Roman town.

There are few vineyards within the urban district of Reims, but a visit to the house of Pommery will reveal one of them, just behind the wall that surrounds the property. This is immediately opposite the 3-star restaurant and hotel of Gérard Boyer, les Crayères, which used to be the home of the former owners of Pommery, the de Polignacs.

The most visible landmark in Reims is its Gothic cathedral and the sight of the early morning sun streaming through its tall windows is unforgettable. The west facade is covered with statuary and many of the original sculptures can be seen in the Palais de Thau next door. The cathedral is also the best place to begin a walking tour of Reims and shops selling a wide selection of Champagne can be found close to the east and west ends of the cathedral. The city suffered considerably during the wars that devastated northeast France from the 16th century onward, none worse than World War One, when only 17 houses were left standing after the bombardments in 1917. The Tourist Office, housed near the cathedral in what appears to be a ruined building, is a reminder of that appalling destruction.

Reims Fact File

The urban geography of the city, a mixture of old and new, can be confusing, and the most famous landmark is the cathedral. A visit to one of the great Champagne houses is another major tourist attraction.

Information

Office de Tourisme
2 rue Guillaume de Machault, 51100 Reims. Tel 03 26 77 45 25; fax 03 26 77 45 27.
The tourist office can organize visits to the cellars of the Champagne houses.

Comité Départemental du Tourisme de la Marne
13 bis rue Carnot, 51000 Châlons-en-Champagne. Tel 03 26 68 37 52; fax 03 26 68 46 45.
Responsible for setting up the *Route touristique du Champagne.* Information on the whole region and can also refer you to smaller local tourist offices.

Champagne Air Show
Champagne Connexion, 15 bis Place St-Nicaise, 51100 Reims. Tel 03 26 68 37 52; fax 03 26 82 48 62.
Balloon excursions in summer over Reims and the vineyards of the Montagne de Reims.

Markets
Place du Boulingrin – Wednesday and Friday mornings

Festivals and Events
The historical and cultural importance of Reims has given rise to several musical, theatrical and historical festivities in the summer: *les fêtes johanniques* (medieval pageantry in late May and early June); *Flâneries musicales d'été* (music festival in July and August); *Rallye des vendanges* (3-day international vintage car rally in mid-September).

Where to Buy Wine
Most Champagne houses will sell their wine both by the bottle and the case. They depend on retailers for most of their sales, so they cannot undercut retail prices to any great extent. But you may get a small discount and the assurance of knowing that the Champagne has been stored in ideal conditions.

La Boutique de la Renomée
Place du Cardinal Luçon, 51100 Reims. Tel 03 26 40 43 85.

La Cave d'Erlon
40 place d'Erlon, 51100 Reims. Tel 03 26 47 44 44.

Les Délices Champenoises
2 rue Rockefeller, 51100 Reims. Tel & fax 03 26 47 35 25.

La Vinocave,
43 place d'Erlon, 51100 Reims. Tel 03 26 40 60 07.

Le Vintage
1 cours Anatole France, 51100 Reims. Tel 03 26 40 40 82.

Where to Stay and Eat

L'Assiette Champenoise (H)(R)
40 avenue Paul Vaillant Couturier, 51430 Reims-Tinqueux. Tel 03 26 84 64 64; fax 03 26 04 15 56. (F)(F)(F)
One of Reims' top restaurants, with a superb wine list, is in fine surroundings just outside the city. The second, less expensive restaurant is by the pool.

Le Boulingrin (R)
48 rue de Mars, 51100 Reims. Tel 03 26 40 96 22; fax 03 26 40 03 92. (F)
Superb traditional brasserie, near the market, with great ambience.

De la Cathédrale (H)
20 rue Libergier, 51100 Reims. Tel 03 26 47 28 46; fax 03 26 88 65 81. (H)
Well situated with ample parking and reasonable prices. Smallish rooms but recently redecorated.

Le Continental (R)
95 place Drouet d'Erlon, 51100 Reims. Tel 03 26 47 01 47; fax 03 26 40 95 60. (F)(F)
On Reims' main pedestrian street. Excellent sea-food; good wine list.

Les Crayères (H)(R)
64 boulevard Henry Vasnier, 51100 Reims. Tel 03 26 82 80 80; fax 03 26 82 65 52. (F)(F)(F)
Reims' top hotel is located in magnificent surroundings on the edge of the city. This is the only 3-star restaurant in Champagne, with a fabulous wine list (at reasonable prices) and excellent *haute cuisine.*

Holiday Inn (H)
46 rue Buirette, 51100 Reims. Tel 03 26 47 56 00; fax 03 26 47 45 75. (F)(F)
Central, modern, comfortable.

Le Café du Palais (R)
Place Myron-Herrick, 51100 Reims. Tel 03 25 47 52 54. (F)
Handy for a drink when visiting the cathedral with a great atmosphere and eclectic décor. Light food and occasional early evening jazz or classical concerts. Closes at 8pm.

Au Petit Bacchus (R)
11 rue de l'Université, 51100 Reims. Tel 03 26 47 10 05; fax 03 26 47 10 05. (F)
Small, friendly wine bar serving good traditional food, including great steak tartare.

Au Petit Comptoir (R)
17 rue de Mars, 51100 Reims. Tel 03 26 40 58 58; fax 03 26 58 44 68. (F)(F)
Small bistro, serving good food and well-chosen wines.

La Vigneraie (R)
14 rue Thillois, 51100 Reims. Tel 03 26 88 67 27; fax 03 26 40 26 67. (F)(F)
This restaurant is the rising star of Reims, with exciting food. Reasonable prices.

Le Vigneron (R)
Place Jamot, 51100 Reims. Tel 03 26 47 00 71; fax 03 26 47 00 71. (F)(F)
Admire the world's biggest collection of Champagne posters while you eat good, traditional food. There is an amazing wine list, with Champagnes going back to the 19th century.

Montagne de Reims

Many of the great Champagne houses proudly indicate which vineyards they own. This Pinot Noir vineyard at Mareuil-sur-Ay belongs to Pommery.

Possibly the best way to start this tour is with a visit to the cellars of one of the great Champagne houses, several of which are based in Reims, for an understanding of how Champagne is made and the fascinating history of the region, much of it linked to particular companies. There is no shortage of houses where, in season, you can simply show up for a fairly standardized group tour, but it is worth calling beforehand at the Office de Tourisme (see p.14), whose staff will be able to help arrange any visit. In many instances, it is better to call ahead and with the more exclusive houses, such as Krug and Roederer, it is worth having an introduction. At most of these large houses English is spoken.

The Tour

The vineyards to the north and west of Reims are situated in an attractive area where they alternate with woods and villages. Starting from Reims, take the N44 north toward Laon, and turn left on to the D26 to St-Thierry shortly after passing under the *autoroute*. You will be able to stay on the D26 for three-quarters of the tour, as it winds its way around the Montagne de Reims.

St-Thierry was certainly one of the first vineyards to be planted by the Romans. As its name implies, it was, and is, the site of a monastery, although this was largely rebuilt as a château in the 18th century. A 12th-century chapel remains, and the village church is well worth looking at, particularly for its entrance porch. Follow the road through Merfy to Chenay, where there is a small *négociant* with good wines, Comte Audoin de Dampierre. Follow signs to Châlons-sur-Vesle, and then Gueux on the former motor-racing circuit of Reims, which used to follow the main roads. The local golf course is here, and visiting players are welcomed. Nearby, on the N31, is an excellent restaurant, la Garenne.

The vineyards become more visible after Gueux, and after passing through the village of Pargny-lès-Reims and crossing the D380 (this is an optional starting point if you want to shorten the tour slightly), you are immediately in the village of Jouy-lès-Reims. About 100m (300yd) down the road, a neon sign on the left informs you of the presence of the cellars of L Aubry Fils, run by two brothers, one of whom speaks English. They will show you their winery, built around a courtyard, and the cellars with low stone vaults. Tasting takes place in a small dining room, using good-quality glasses, and the wines are superbly fruity and stylish. Don't miss the rosé, which is an unusually

TOUR SUMMARY

This tour starts in Reims and traverses the area known as the Montagne de Reims, which is, in fact, just a ridge of land rising to 300m (1000ft). This top-quality Champagne area with a string of famous wine villages curves in an enormous horseshoe between Reims and Épernay.

Distance covered   150km (90 miles) including detours.

Time needed   7 hours to do the tour full justice, but it could be shortened to half a day.

Terrain   The roads are, for the most part, narrow and twisting, but the tour follows a well-signed *route touristique du Champagne*.

Hotels   Reims and Épernay have the most choice, but there are one or two in the wine villages.

Restaurants   Places to eat are few and far between in the small villages so it is worth planning where to stop for a meal and booking ahead. Most of the better restaurants are slightly off the wine route. The wooded hills above the vineyards provide plenty of attractive picnic sites.

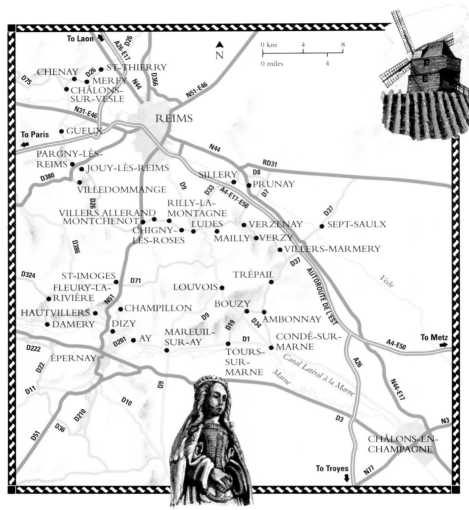

To Laon

CHENAY
MERFY
CHÂLONS-SUR-VESLE
ST-THIERRY

REIMS

To Paris   GUEUX

PARGNY-LÈS-REIMS
JOUY-LÈS-REIMS
VILLEDOMMANGE

SILLERY
PRUNAY

RILLY-LA-MONTAGNE
VILLERS ALLERAND
MONTCHENOT
CHIGNY-LES-ROSES
LUDES
MAILLY
VERZENAY
VERZY
SEPT-SAULX
VILLERS-MARMERY

ST-IMOGES
FLEURY-LA-RIVIÈRE
HAUTVILLERS
DAMERY
DIZY
CHAMPILLON
LOUVOIS
BOUZY
TRÉPAIL
AMBONNAY

MAREUIL-SUR-AY
AY
ÉPERNAY
TOURS-SUR-MARNE
CONDÉ-SUR-MARNE

To Metz

CHÂLONS-EN-CHAMPAGNE

To Troyes

0 km   4   8
0 miles   4

N

Map illustrations: (above) the historic windmill at Verzenay now owned by the Champagne house of Heidsieck Monopole; (below) statue on the church at Villedommange.

interesting example of this type of Champagne. If it is lunch time, there is a restaurant back on the main road called le Pargny. Do not expect *haute cuisine* or elaborate décor, but you will receive a friendly welcome and fresh food at unbeatable prices; and the wine list is short but informative.

Next along the road is Villedommange, a hillside village clearly devoted to Champagne. It is worth turning off the D26 to reach it, since you will get a good view of the sweep of vineyards, topped by woods, that look toward Reims. When you reach the N51, turn left, which will bring you immediately to Montchenot and le Grand Cerf, one of Champagne's most pleasant country auberges, which is blessed with a superb wine list. This junction is particularly dangerous, so cross it very carefully and drive through Villers Allerand. Just out of the village, at the top of the hill on the right-hand side, there is an extraordinary museum called la Ferme des Bermonts, which is devoted to wine and wine-making. It is not well signposted, so go slowly.

Jean-Pierre Liégent, whose son Hervé runs le Vigneron, one of Reims' most enjoyable restaurants, has over the years collected a huge number of tools and objects of all descriptions linked not only to the Champagne region but also to other wines and to bread-making. By appointment, M. Liégent will show you around and explain the use of every object. He doesn't speak much English but he is a natural communicator and his gestures are eloquent.

The village of Rilly-la-Montagne follows on immediately. The grower Marc Chauvet is based across the road from the church, curiously known locally as a cathedral. At Chigny-les-Roses the Cattier family have been making Champagne since 1763 and produce one of Champagne's very rare single-vineyard wines, the Clos du Moulin, which is within the neighbouring commune of Ludes. Their cellars are among the deepest in Champagne and the vaults are carved in different styles. It is worth branching off the D26 at Ludes and heading for the village of Sillery, where there is a good restaurant, le Relais de Sillery, and an interesting grower, François Secondé, whose wines are highly individual, particularly an Extra-Brut free of any dosage. Sillery was for centuries one of Champagne's most famous wine villages, and it holds the status of Grand Cru today, along with 16 other villages.

Back on the D26, head for Mailly-Champagne, where the local co-operative, called Mailly Grand Cru, is unusual in that it makes wines only from this village. Its cellars, dug out by hand by its members, are very deep and are worth visiting, and the tasting room looks out over the vineyards. At Verzenay the windmill is a famous local landmark. It's worth stopping and walking around it – the view over the vineyards is impressive and, in fact, the windmill was used as an observation post during World War One. In an area where, to a great extent, the vineyards are owned by the large houses from Reims, Michel Arnould and Jean Lallement are two growers making excellent wines from tiny vineyards in the best part of Verzenay. The restaurant here, Au Chant des Galipes, is a good place for lunch.

The road on to Verzy twists through the vineyards along the edge of the woods, and the shallowness of the topsoil over the chalk rock is visible in several places . You may notice metal signboards of different colours in the vineyards. These are markers for the helicopters that are sometimes used to spray small strips of vines, since the vineyard holdings are, for the most part, divided into numerous small plots. In Verzy the grower Juillet-Lallement is worth visiting. On the way out of the village, heading toward Villers-Marmery, look out for a sign on the right indicating the Faux de Verzy. These twisted beech trees (*Fagus sylvatica tortuosa*) are a botanical curiosity and worth seeing.

On the north-facing part of the Montagne de Reims the grapes need every bit of available sun to ripen. Most of the vines here are on almost flat lower slopes and so can benefit from the cool but long summer day's sun. The wooded ridges also help shelter the vineyards from the harsh winter climate.

From here the road plunges toward the valley, before running south to Villers-Marmery, which, with its neighbour Trépail, is unusual in that its vineyards are almost entirely planted to Chardonnay in an area dominated by Pinot Noir. The Margaine family are typical of many growers here as they use mainly Chardonnay in their blend of Champagne. From here it's a short distance down the valley to the village of Sept-Saulx on the banks of the river Vesle where there is a welcoming auberge called le Cheval Blanc. The food is fine and the wine list even better. This is also a quiet place to stay if you need to break the tour.

Otherwise, continue through Trépail to the pretty village of Ambonnay on an old Roman road, where the view is spectacular as the landscape opens out to the upper Marne Valley. Some of Ambonnay's houses are decorated with fine, wrought-iron signs and an old wine press can be seen on the left as you enter the village. As well as several good growers who welcome visitors, there is also a good restaurant, the Auberge St-Vincent and named after the patron saint of winemakers. You can also taste different Champagnes and see exhibitions at the Palette de Bacchus.

At Ambonnay decide whether you are going to visit Châlons-en-Champagne, or Châlons-sur-Marne as it used to be called until 1995. An attractive town, with a cathedral that blends Romanesque and Gothic styles, it is the home of at least one good Champagne house, Joseph Perrier, and is the administrative capital of the Marne department.

War cemeteries scattered throughout the wine villages are a reminder of the terrible fighting that took place in the Montagne de Reims vineyards during World War One's bloody Battle of the Marne. This one is at Villers-Marmery.

To continue touring the Montagne de Reims, turn right in Ambonnay to Bouzy, whose extensive vineyards are famous for the red Coteaux Champenois wine called Bouzy Rouge. This is one of those wines that is the victim of its fame, and it is quite hard to find a drinkable one, let alone one that is worth the price demanded. But some excellent Champagne is produced here, including wines used in blends by the big houses and those made on the spot by growers such as Paul Bara, E Barnault or Jean Vesselle.

From Bouzy, it's a short detour right to admire the Ch. de Louvois through its gates. Then continue to Tours-sur-Marne, home of Laurent-Perrier. Laurent-Perrier is one of the few Grande Marque Champagne houses located adjacent to its vineyards and where the whole process, from vineyard to finished bottle, can be seen in one go. It's worth making an appointment in advance as the Champagne is very good, and the tour informative.

From Tours, follow the D1 road, which leads along the Marne canal to Mareuil-sur-Ay. As you come to the village, the house of Billecart-Salmon can be seen on the roadside to the right. This is one of Champagne's smaller top-quality houses still owned by the family, and their wines are highly recommended. The excellent firm of Philipponnat is also

based here. Next along the route is Ay, the third town of Champagne, after Reims and Épernay, and several excellent medium-sized houses, such as Bollinger, Deutz and Gosset, are based here. A tasting and visit at Bollinger, the most traditional of Champagne houses, is unforgettable, but be sure to make an appointment first.

Right by the church in Ay is the home of an admirable small producer called Gatinois. Here you will be shown into a comfortable living room, decorated with paintings of the Champagne vineyards, and offered a series of well-made wines from the best parts of Ay. The empty bottles on display here from other wine areas and countries shows that, unlike many other Champagne growers, Gatinois has a worldwide interest in wine. The Champagnes are full-bodied and ripe, with tantalizingly spicy aromas, and the still red Coteaux Champenois is one of the best in Champagne.

Although Ay has its Musée Champenois it is strangely bereft of restaurants, but then Épernay, luckily, is just across the river. The final leg of this tour leads us to Dizy – virtually an extension of Épernay – on the right bank of the Marne. Along the stretch of road between Ay and Dizy it's easy to spot the chalky subsoil which is found in all the best Champagne vineyards. Dizy is worth visiting to discover one of Champagne's better and lesser-known houses, Jacquesson et Fils. Like several other quality producers, the Chiquet brothers who run Jacquesson believe in a traditional approach to making Champagne, which involves some of the wine being made in oak tuns, or *foudres*. The buildings, set in a walled garden, are very attractive.

From Dizy it's only a few minutes across the Marne to Épernay, or turn uphill, toward the main N51 that leads back to Reims.

The Clos des Goisses is a beautifully sited vineyard on a slope above the Marne canal at Mareuil-sur-Ay. The steep, south-facing vineyard belongs exclusively to Philipponnat and is of high Grand Cru quality.

Montagne de Reims Fact File

'Mountain' is a generous description of this curve of hillside that runs between Reims and Épernay, since its highest point is under 300m (1000ft) above sea level. On its slopes are some of the oldest and best wine-producing villages of Champagne.

Information

Comité Départemental du Tourisme de la Marne
See p.14.

Office de Tourisme de Châlons-en-Champagne
3 quai des Arts, 51000 Châlons-en-Champagne. Tel 03 26 65 17 89; fax 03 26 21 72 92.

Point Information Tourisme
Mairie d'Ay, place de la Mairie, 51160 Ay. Tel 02 26 56 92 10. Tourist office open in summer.

Musée Champenois
Maison Laurain, place de la Mairie, 51160 Ay. Tel 03 26 55 18 90.
Small Champagne museum in a 16th-century grower's house. Also a short film explaining the Champagne method as well as wine-tasting and sales. (See Maison Laurain right.)

La Ferme des Bermonts
51500 Rilly-la-Montagne. Tel 03 26 97 66 50.
Owned by Jean-Pierre Liegent, this remarkable and unusual museum is devoted to viticulture and the making of Champagne, as well as wheat and bread-making. By appointment only.

Markets

Ay – Friday morning

Festivals and Events

The *Fête de St-Vincent* is celebrated in most of the wine villages on 22 January. Every even-numbered year, on the first weekend in July, Ay holds a 2-day festival with Portes Ouvertes, or open days when producers throw open their doors and hold tastings for visitors, tastings and pageantry (tel 03 2656 92 10). In July the villages on the *route touristique du Champagne* hold special events and exhibitions (tel 03 26 55 16 15).

Where to Buy Wine

Buy from the producers in the villages as there are few wine shops outside Reims and Épernay.
Maison Laurain
2 rue Roger Sondag, 51160 Ay. Tel 03 26 55 18 90.
Small wine museum (see Musée Champenois left) and producer also selling a range of other Champagnes, mainly from Ay and the locality.

Nicolas
41 place de la République, 51000 Châlons-en-Champagne. Tel 03 26 68 52 84.
Part of the well-known chain of wine shops and therefore has a wide selection.

La Palette de Bacchus
12 rue St-Vincent, 51150 Ambonnay. Tel 03 26 57 07 87.
Taste different Champagnes at the bar from Easter to October. Good selection sold by the bottle.

Where to Stay and Eat

Hôtel d'Angleterre Ⓗ Ⓡ
19 place Monseigneur Tissier, 51000 Châlons-en-Champagne. Tel 03 26 68 21 51; fax 03 26 70 51 67. Ⓕ Ⓕ Ⓕ
Comfortable, spacious rooms and the best restaurant in town.

Au Carillon Gourmand Ⓡ
15 bis place Monseigneur Tissier, 51000 Châlons-en-Champagne. Tel 03 26 64 45 07; fax 03 26 66 92 31. Ⓕ
Good country food.

Au Chant des Galipes Ⓡ
2 rue Chanzy, 51380 Verzy. Tel 03 26 97 91 40. Ⓕ Ⓕ
Next to the town hall, this restaurant serves traditional recipes with modern touches.

Le Cheval Blanc Ⓗ Ⓡ
Rue du Moulin, 51400 Sept-Saulx. Tel 03 26 03 90 27; fax 03 26 03 97 09. Ⓕ Ⓕ

Quiet hotel in a garden with bright, modernized rooms and excellent breakfasts. Classic cuisine and a well-chosen wine list.

La Garenne Ⓡ
N31, Gueux, 51370 Champigny-sur-Vesle. Tel 03 26 08 26 62; fax 03 26 84 24 13. Ⓕ Ⓕ Ⓕ
Overlooking Reims' old racing circuit, this restaurant has one of the region's best young chefs. Excellent classic food with a touch of fantasy and good wines.

Golf de Gueux Ⓡ
Gueux. Tel 03 26 05 46 11; fax 03 26 05 46 19. Ⓕ Ⓕ
Delightful tiny château surrounded by trees; the dining room looks out over the 18-hole golf course which is open to non-members. Fine Champagne available by the glass or bottle at reasonable prices.

Le Grand Cerf Ⓡ
N51, Montchenot, 51500 Villers Allerand. Tel 03 26 97 60 07; fax 03 26 97 64 24. Ⓕ Ⓕ Ⓕ
Fine auberge with a shaded terrace for the summer and excellent food. Top-class wine list and a very good *sommelier*.

Le Pargny Ⓡ
36 route de Dormans, 51390 Pargny-lès-Reims. Tel 03 26 49 20 00. Ⓕ
Simple restaurant in the village café serving wholesome food.

Le Relais de Sillery Ⓡ
51500 Sillery. Tel 03 26 49 10 11; fax 03 26 49 12 07. Ⓕ Ⓕ
Attractive restaurant serving good traditional food.

La Touraine Champenoise Ⓗ Ⓡ
51150 Tours-sur-Marne. Tel 03 26 58 91 93; fax 03 26 58 95 47. Ⓕ
Simple canalside establishment with friendly ambience serving local dishes.

Auberge St-Vincent Ⓗ Ⓡ
51150 Ambonnay. Tel 03 26 57 01 98; fax 03 26 57 81 48. Ⓕ Ⓕ
Village inn with simple, bedrooms and outstanding food.

Wines and Wine Villages

Although most of the major Champagne houses are based in Reims and Épernay, hundreds of growers in the wine villages are increasingly making their own Champagne rather than selling their grapes to a Champagne house or the local co-operative. These villages were severely battered during World War One, so do not expect too much architectural splendour.

Ambonnay (Grand Cru, Pinot Noir) Pretty village situated at the junction between the Montagne de Reims and the upper Marne Valley.
Best producers: BEAUFORT, *Coutier*, ÉGLY-OURIET, SOUTIRAN.

Ay (Grand Cru, Pinot Noir) Ay used to be a walled town and several kings owned vineyards here, including Henri IV of France and Henry VIII of England. There is also a small wine museum.
Best producers: BOLLINGER, DEUTZ, GATINOIS, GOSSET.

Bouzy (Grand Cru, Pinot Noir) Lying at the foot of a great slope of top-quality vineyards, Bouzy is one of Champagne's best villages. Some of the best still red Coteaux Champenois wines come from here.
Best producers: BARA, BARNAULT, *Hubert Beaufort*, JEAN VESSELLE.

Châlons-en-Champagne
This town with many fine buildings was an important centre of the Champagne trade in the 19th century.
Best producer: JOSEPH PERRIER.

Chenay (Other Cru 84%, Pinot Noir) Surrounded by woods this peaceful village has a handsome 12th-century church and 4 fountains.
Best producer: *Dampierre*.

Chigny-les-Roses (Premier Cru 94%, Pinot Noir) 'Les Roses' was added to the village name when a rose garden was planted here early in the 20th century. Mme Pommery, a famous 19th-century Champagne widow who ran Pommery after her husband's death, lived here.
Best producers: CATTIER, *Lassalle*.

One of the most traditional Champagne houses is the family-owned firm of Bollinger, based at Ay.

Dizy (Premier Cru 95%, Pinot Noir) Across the Marne from Épernay, this village has several good houses and growers.
Best producers: CHIQUET, JACQUESSON.

Jouy-lès-Reims (Premier Cru 90%, Pinot Meunier) The church has a fine stained glass window.
Best producer: AUBRY.

Ludes (Premier Cru 94%, Pinot Meunier) The attractive location is somewhat spoilt by Canard-Duchêne's factory-like building.
Best producer: GAIDOZ-FORGET.

Mailly-Champagne (Grand Cru, Pinot Noir) Visit the local chalk quarries to see the famous brilliant white subsoil of this area of Champagne.
Best producer: MAILLY GRAND CRU.

Mareuil-sur-Ay (Premier Cru 99%, Pinot Noir) Philipponnat's famous Clos des Goisses vineyard borders the Marne canal.
Best producers: BILLECART-SALMON, PHILIPPONNAT.

Rilly-la-Montagne (Premier Cru 94%, Pinot Noir) Nestling under Mont Joli, this village is home to la Ferme des Bermonts, an unusual private museum.
Best producers: CHAUVET, *Germain*, VILMART.

Sillery (Grand Cru, Pinot Noir) Sillery has a long and glorious history as a wine village.
Best producer: SECONDÉ.

St-Thierry (Other Cru 87%, Pinot Meunier) There has been a monastery here since the 6th century; the church dates from the 12th century.

Tours-sur-Marne (Grand Cru, Pinot Noir; Premier Cru 90%, Chardonnay) Farming is as important as viticulture in this village located on the edge of the Montagne de Reims.
Best producer: LAURENT-PERRIER.

Verzenay (Grand Cru, Pinot Noir) One of the best wine villages of the Montagne de Reims and famous for its windmill, owned by Heidsieck Monopole, a local landmark which can be visited.
Best producers: ARNOULD, LALLEMENT, *Pithois*.

Verzy (Grand Cru, Pinot Noir) Old wine village near the extraordinary wood of twisted beech trees, known as les Faux de Verzy, which makes an excellent spot for picnics.
Best producer: JUILLET-LALLEMENT.

Villedommange (Premier Cru 90%, Pinot Meunier) Attractive hillside village dominated by its 12th-century church and surrounded by vineyards. From here there is a sweeping view of the northern part of the Montagne de Reims.
Best producer: *Bardoux*.

Villers-Marmery (Premier Cru 95%, Chardonnay) Unlike the rest of the Montagne de Reims, this village specializes in in Chardonnay.
Best producer: MARGAINE.

After the grapes have been harvested in Champagne, usually in mid-October, the *vigneron* begins the slow work of tidying up. The vine's longer shoots are trimmed off, conserving the plant's energy for the long winter ahead, and the prunings are burnt in the vineyard. This great sweep of Pinot Noir vines, above the village of Bouzy on the south-eastern side of the Montagne de Reims, contains some of Champagne's finest vineyards. Bouzy is also well known for its better than average still red Coteaux Champenois. The Montagne de Reims is a large upland between Reims and Épernay and the plateau on top is heavily forested, leaving the slopes on its northern, eastern and southern sides to the vineyards. It is bordered to the south by the Marne Valley. This is the furthest north of the various Champagne zones and is mostly planted with Pinot Noir, which is well suited to the long ripening period of a cool wine region.

Épernay

Although Épernay calls itself the capital of Champagne, it is a modest provincial town which happens to be the home of some of Champagne's major houses, and of the wine-governing body, the Comité Interprofessionel de Champagne (CIVC). Situated on the Marne, Épernay used to be the port from which wines from Champagne were shipped downriver and, via Paris, overseas. The three most famous sub-regions of the Champagne vineyards (Montagne de Reims, Vallée de la Marne and Côte des Blancs) converge on Epernay, and it is this strategic location that has given it its role. The town is surrounded by vineyards, and it even has a vineyard of its own, rated at 88 per cent.

Épernay does not have the wealth of attractions that Reims offers and a walk around the town can be concentrated on one small area along and around the prestigious avenue de Champagne with its opulent 19th-century buildings. This is where most of the town's Champagne houses are located and beneath these streets over 100km (60 miles) of underground cellars hold enormous stocks of bottles in which Champagne is slowly maturing. De Castellane's tower is a landmark of Épernay, and their buildings house many interesting collections, including labels. The Office de Tourisme, at the west end of the avenue de Champagne, is the best starting point for a tour, as it provides information about the houses that can be visited. On the other side of the avenue is Moët et Chandon, one of the oldest established houses and also by far the largest. The tour by multilingual guides is excellent and clearly illustrates the complex processes needed to make Champagne.

Moët et Chandon's de luxe Champagne is named after the Benedictine cellarer monk, Dom Pérignon, whose statue greets visitors at the entrance to its headquarters in Épernay.

A little further along the avenue de Champagne are Perrier-Jouët and de Venoge, and nearby are Pol Roger and Alfred Gratien. A visit to either of these two houses will give a more individual idea of Champagne. Pol Roger is famous for having been Sir Winston Churchill's favourite Champagne, and the premises still retain a decidedly British atmosphere. Its non-vintage is one of the most reliable in Champagne and has a perfect balance between freshness and rounded flavours; there is also a rare collection of old vintage Champagnes going back to the 19th century.

Alfred Gratien is a small Champagne house belonging to Gratien et Meyer, the Loire firm making sparkling Saumur, and pursuing a high-quality, extremely traditional approach. An appointment is necessary, and since there is every chance that you will be shown around by the cellarmaster himself, it is better to speak French. Do not expect luxurious reception rooms – this is very much a working cellar underneath the offices.

Épernay Fact File

A convenient stopping point, the prosperous town of Épernay is home to a number of important Champagne houses. Most of the town dates from the 19th century, but it was extensively rebuilt after the devastating bombardments of World War One.

Information

Office de Tourisme d'Épernay
7 avenue de Champagne, 51200 Épernay. Tel 03 26 53 33 00; fax 03 26 51 95 22.
Will arrange visits to Champagne houses, which can be conducted in English, as well as a guided tour of the town. Also provides help with accommodation.

Comité Interprofessionnel du Vin de Champagne
5 rue Henri Martin, 51200 Épernay. Tel 03 26 51 17 20; fax 03 26 55 19 79.
The CIVC is the official body that oversees most aspects of the production of Champagne. It provides technical information on Champagne and also addresses of houses to visit.

Musée de Préhistoire et d'Archéologie and Musée du Vin de Champagne
13 avenue de Champagne, 51200 Épernay. Tel 03 26 51 90 31.
The splendid Château Perrier houses the Musée de Préhistoire et d'Archéologie, which holds the finest archaeological collection in France outside Paris. It also contains a museum devoted to the wines of Champagne, which is currently undergoing a much needed renovation.

Markets

Halle St-Thibault, rue Gallice (on the road to Sézanne) – Saturday morning
Place Auban Moët (in the town centre) – Sunday morning

Festivals and Events

Vit'eff, a trade fair dealing with technical equipment for making Champagne, is held every 2 years in June; it is open to the general public. The *Fête de St-Vincent* takes place on 22 January. December brings a Christmas market. The dates for some of the events vary from one year to another, so it is best to check with the Office de Tourisme.

Where to Buy Wine

As elsewhere in Champagne, most Champagne houses will sell their wine by the bottle or the case. They depend on retailers for the major part of their sales, so they cannot undercut retail prices to any great extent. But you may get a small discount and the assurance of knowing that the wines have been stored in ideal conditions.

Achille Princier
9 rue Jean Chandon Moët, 51200 Épernay. Tel 03 26 54 04 06; fax 03 26 59 16 90.

La Cave Salvatori
11 rue Flodard, 51200 Épernay. Tel 03 26 55 32 32.
This small shop has a wide selection of Grande Marque and other Champagnes.

Le Domaine des Crus
2 rue Henri Dunant, 51200 Épernay. Tel 03 26 54 18 60.
Slightly out of the town centre, this is the largest wine shop in Épernay. It stocks a wide range of Champagnes, including a selection of gift boxes, and also souvenirs related to Champagne.

Where to Stay and Eat

Les Berceaux (H)(R)
13 rue des Berceaux, 51200 Épernay. Tel 03 26 55 28 84; fax 03 26 55 10 36. (F)(R)
A new chef for this pillar of Épernay's restaurant scene should give it a fresh lease of life. The restaurant serves classic food and there is a wine bar next door.

La Briqueterie (H)(R)
Route de Sézanne, 51530 Vinay. Tel 03 26 59 99 99; fax 03 26 59 92 10. (F)(F)(F)

This refined, modern hotel has large bedrooms and marble bathrooms. There are 2 swimming pools. The excellent restaurant serves classic cuisine and has a magnificent wine list.

Hôtel de Champagne (H)
30 rue Eugène Mercier, 51200 Épernay. Tel 03 26 53 10 60; fax 03 26 51 94 63. (F)
Located near the Champagne houses, this simple hotel provides breakfast but has no restaurant.

Chez Pierrot (R)
16 rue de la Fauvette, 51200 Épernay. Tel 03 26 55 16 93; fax 03 26 54 51 30. (F)(F)
Small, family-run restaurant with friendly atmosphere and serving local dishes. The Champagnes are mainly from small growers in the Épernay area.

Hôtel de la Cloche (H)(R)
3–5 place Mendès France, 51200 Épernay. Tel 03 26 55 24 05; fax 03 26 51 88 05. (F)
This attractive building is located on a small square. Inside, the rooms resemble those of an inexpensive chain and the ones facing the square can be noisy.

La Grillade (R)
16 rue de Reims, 51200 Épernay. Tel 03 26 55 44 22. (F)(F)
The menu includes excellent grilled fish and meat. The short, well-chosen wine list has wines from all over France.

La Table Kobus (R)
3 rue du Dr Rousseau, 51200 Épernay. Tel 03 26 51 53 53; fax 03 26 58 42 68. (F)(F)
This very pleasant bistro serves wholesome food. The wine list contains keenly priced Champagnes.

La Terrasse (R)
7 quai de Marne, 51200 Épernay. Tel 03 26 55 26 05; fax 03 26 55 33 79. (F)
Although the décor is not idyllic, the restaurant is in a pleasant location by the river. Prices vary according to the menu chosen and there is a decent wine list.

The village of Hautvillers, perched above its vineyards, is much visited as the mythical birthplace of sparkling Champagne. Dom Pérignon, the monk credited with inventing the Champagne method, lived at the Benedictine abbey here.

Map illustrations: (left) wrought-iron sign in Hautvillers; (right) the village of Cumières across the river Marne.

Vallée de la Marne

The vineyards on this tour run west from Épernay to just beyond Château-Thierry, with few interruptions. They are strung out along both sides of the river Marne, generally on the hillside. The road alternately runs along the valley or zigzags through the vineyards.

The Tour

Leave Épernay on the N3, heading for Château-Thierry. After about 5km (3 miles), look for signs on the left to Boursault, and take the first turn (the D222). This runs past the Ch. de Boursault, which is surrounded by walls and woods but is visible from the road. This 19th-century château, designed in the Loire Valley Renaissance style, was built by Mme Clicquot, Champagne's most famous widow. It no longer belongs to the house of Veuve Clicquot-Ponsardin, and is not open to the public, but the present owners make a decent Champagne which you can taste near the house while enjoying the view.

If you left Épernay late in the morning and are now ready for lunch, there is a simple but good restaurant in Boursault called du Marronnier. Another, le Petit Pressoir,

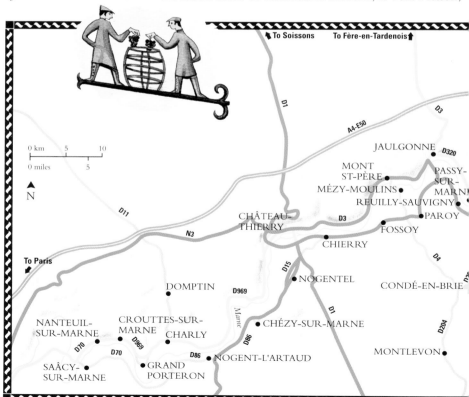

is run by a local grower and is open only at weekends. After Boursault, stay on the upper road until you reach Oeuilly, since it will give you a close look at the vineyards, which slope spectacularly down to the river. Oeuilly is an enterprising village. Tarlant, its best Champagne producer, also has *chambres d'hôte*, and a nearby grower's house has been converted into a museum called la Maison Champenoise. The church is interesting, and you can visit the old school house, an excellent way of seeing what life was like a century ago.

Back on the N3, continue to the small town of Dormans, then branch away from the river toward Condé-en-Brie, on the D41. The Ch. de Condé, which is privately owned but can be visited, is remarkably unspoiled and unusually full of 18th-century furniture. The village also has a fine covered market place. From here, the D4 takes you back to the Marne along a charming little valley with some vineyards on the right-hand side. If you are now ready for a very good meal, you will have to turn right, back toward Épernay, for a couple of kilometres to the village of Reuilly-Sauvigny and the 1-star Relais de Reuilly, overlooking the Marne.

Otherwise, turn left toward Château-Thierry and carry on to Fossoy, where signs will lead you down into the village and to the house of Dehu Père et Fils. Here a small, beautifully kept museum shows the full process of vine-

TOUR SUMMARY

Beginning in Épernay, this is the longest of the Champagne tours, especially if you continue to the western end of the vineyards beyond Château-Thierry. Growers and sights are more scattered here than elsewhere in Champagne.

Distance covered 150km (90 miles) including detours.

Time needed 7 hours.

Terrain Apart from the first stretch on the left bank, the roads are fairly empty, since the *autoroute* takes most of the through traffic.

Hotels Although there are one or two good hotels in the wine villages, there is little choice of accommodation except in Épernay.

Restaurants Local restaurants of varying price categories offer an adequate choice, and there are plenty of opportunities for picnicking.

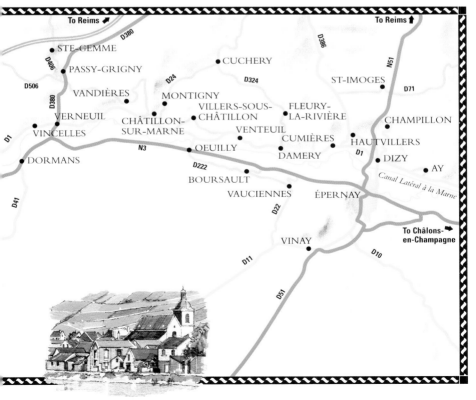

growing and Champagne-making. There are also a few vines in the garden so that you can see the differences between the three grape varieties – Pinot Noir, Chardonnay and Pinot Meunier. After a visit, you can taste the wines, which are well made for Dehu by the co-operative at Château-Thierry, whose own brand, Pannier, is highly recommended. Château-Thierry is only a few kilometres away, and you can choose either to cross the river to visit the co-operative now or wait until the return trip and continue down the left bank to Nogent-l'Artaud.

The western extremity of the Champagne vineyards is at Nanteuil-sur-Marne, about 20km (12 miles) beyond Château-Thierry. As you drive west, the vineyards become almost exclusive to the right bank. At Saâcy-sur-Marne you reach their limit, and the vineyards on the left before you come into the village are the last. Turn right, cross the Marne, and head back toward Château-Thierry through the villages of Nanteuil and Crouttes-sur-Marne.

Before you reach Charly, watch out for signposts to Grand Porteron, which lies off the D969 on the right. The winery here, Baron-Albert, has nothing to do with aristocracy but results from the association of two families called Albert and Baron. You will find a friendly welcome and some straightforward, well-made Champagnes. Take a look at the cellars, which were dug by hand by the owner's father.

Drive on into Charly and look closely for the sign for Baron-Fuenté (another member of the Baron family married a Spanish woman, Dolores Fuenté). This leads you through a porch into a courtyard where there is a clean new tasting room. All the wines are good, supple and fruity and the vintages will keep well. Baron-Fuenté use a balanced blend from the three Champagne grapes, which have been planted on steep, often south-facing slopes.

Continue to Château-Thierry for an interesting visit to the large cellars of Pannier. Modern equipment and the impressive low-vaulted cellars dug out of the hill above the town combine to produce a range of excellent Champagnes that deserve to be better known. If you need a break, go north toward Soissons on the D1 for about 2km (1 mile) to the Hôtel Île de France, which has a good restaurant.

Heading toward Châtillon on the D3, you follow the meanders of the Marne. At Mont St-Père, look across the river to the splendid large church of Mézy-Moulins. Soon you come to Jaulgonne, where the slopes are so steep that, unusually for Champagne, the vines have been planted in terraces. On the inside bend of the river, the peaceful village of Passy-sur-Marne is home to the Servaux family who make reliable Champagne. At Verneuil you can turn left on the D380 up an attractive little valley with vineyards on either side that leads to Passy-Grigny and Ste-Gemme. The

From the village of Châtillon-sur-Marne there is a commanding view of the Marne Valley. Crowning the hilltop is an 18m- (60ft-) high statue of the 11th-century Pope Urban II who came from the area.

road back to the Marne takes you to Vandières, where the houses huddle around a Romanesque church with a 12th-century porch. Châtillon-sur-Marne is a former fortified village, whose position commands the Marne Valley and the smaller Cuchery Valley. In the village square are shops and the only decent restaurant for a long way, la Porte Oubliée.

Across the valley lies Montigny. Take the steep road that leads to this tiny hamlet and halfway up the hill, on the right, are the cellars of Charlier et Fils, with wooden barrels standing outside. This is a delightful family concern, friendly and enterprising, which has thought carefully about how to interest visitors. Original ideas include a map of the Champagne vineyards in the form of a flower garden, magnificent carved barrels in the cellar, and the sale of other local produce to complement their Champagnes, which are of good quality, in a full, vinous style. In neighbouring Villers-sous-Châtillon, entirely devoted to the production of Champagne, is another excellent family company, Jacky Charpentier, where the wines are well-knit, with a refreshing tang to them.

Take the D1 through Venteuil, then turn left at Damery to Fleury-la-Rivière, which stands in a sea of vines with roses planted at the end of each row. It is worth visiting the local co-operative, Arnoult, for its frescos, which tell the story of Champagne. There are good conducted tours in English. Back in Damery, cross the bridge and refresh yourself at le Bateau Lavoir, which has a decent wine list, straightforward food and is in a perfect setting on the banks of the Marne.

The last leg of this tour includes Cumières and Hautvillers. Cumières is one of the rare villages in Champagne celebrated for its red wine. Look out for le Caveau, a restaurant hewn out of the chalk. It serves typical local dishes and Cumières wine. Hautvillers, sheltering under the walls of the restored abbey now owned by Moët et Chandon, must be one of the most attractive Champagne villages. It is much visited as the mythical birthplace of sparkling Champagne, although the tales told about the 'inventor's' role of the 17th-century monk Dom Pérignon are notoriously apocryphal and tainted with commercial interest.

Wander around the village to admire the intricate wrought-iron signs indicating the trade practised in various houses and visit one of the local growers, such as Locret-Lachaud. If you have made a prior appointment with Moët you can visit parts of the abbey but you don't need one to picnic on the edge of the abbey gardens. Then you can either return to Épernay or treat yourself to a well-earned dinner at the Royal Champagne hotel at Champillon, where the superb views over the Premier Cru vineyards and the Marne Valley will allow you to meditate on the river you have just explored.

Many of the old stone houses in Hautvillers are decorated with colourful wrought-iron signs.

Vallée de la Marne Fact File

The Marne Valley stretches from Châlons in the east to beyond Château-Thierry in the west. In fact, the western extremity of the vineyards is nearer to Paris than to Reims.

Information

Comité Départemental du Tourisme de l'Aisne
1 rue St-Martin, Laon. Tel 03 23 27 76 76; fax 03 23 27 76 89.

Syndicat d'Initiative
11 rue de la Vallée, 12400 Château-Thierry. Tel 03 23 83 10 14; fax 03 23 83 14 74.

La Maison Champenoise
51480 Oeuilly. Tel 03 26 58 30 60.
Typical 17th-century Champagne grower's house, and also offering Champagne tasting.

Musée de l'Outillage Champenoise
Le Moulin d'en Haut, 51700 Dormans. Tel 03 26 58 80 30.
Interesting small museum.

Markets

Charly-sur-Marne – Thursday morning
Château-Thierry – Tuesday and Friday mornings
Dormans – Saturday morning

Festivals and Events

Cumières' *Foire de la St-Jean* takes place on the Saturday nearest to 24 June and Château-Thierry's festival of *St-Jean de la Fontaine* on the last weekend in June. The *Foire de la vigne* is held in Charly on the 4th Sunday in September and the *Foire de St-Crépin* in Dormans on the Saturday nearest to 25 October.

Where to Buy Wine

Most growers are only too happy to sell their wines to passers-by and there are few wine shops in the villages. One exception is the Maison de Vigneron restaurant.

Where to Stay and Eat

Le Bateau Lavoir Ⓡ
3 rue de Port-au-Bois, 51480 Damery. Tel 03 26 58 40 88. Ⓕ
Simple restaurant in a pleasant setting by the river.

Le Caveau Ⓡ
Rue de la Coopérative, 51480 Cumières. Tel 03 26 59 83 23. Ⓕ
Excellent local food in a cellar.

De la Chapotte Ⓡ
51480 Vauciennes. Tel 03 26 58 44 10. Ⓕ
This restaurant, in a farmhouse overlooking the Marne on the D222 road from Épernay, serves substantial country food with a local flavour.

Chez Tarlant Ⓗ
51480 Oeuilly. Tel 03 26 58 30 60. Ⓕ
Bed and breakfast on offer next to the home of a friendly grower, who is a great source of information on the region.

Le Cygne d'Argent Ⓗ Ⓡ
02310 Domptin. Tel 03 23 70 79 90; fax 03 23 70 79 90. Ⓕ Ⓕ
Simple hotel but the restaurant serves well-prepared local and classic food. There is a decent wine list.

Château de Fère Ⓗ Ⓡ
02130 Fère-en-Tardenois. Tel 03 23 82 21 13; fax 03 23 82 37 81. Ⓕ Ⓕ Ⓕ
The region's top hotel 22km (13½ miles) north-east of Château-Thierry on the D967. Beautiful 16th-century building set in parkland. Fine classic food and excellent wine list.

Hôtel Île de France Ⓗ Ⓡ
Route de Soissons, 02400 Château-Thierry. Tel 03 23 69 10 12; fax 03 23 83 49 70. Ⓕ Ⓕ
Just north of town, this hotel has great views over the local countryside, reasonable prices and a wide range of menus.

Jean de la Fontaine Ⓡ
10 rue Filoirs, 02400 Château-Thierry. Tel 03 23 83 63 89; fax 03 23 83 20 54. Ⓕ Ⓕ
Good traditional restaurant tucked away in a side street.

Maison du Vigneron Ⓡ
N51, 51160 St-Imoges. Tel 03 26 52 88 00; fax 03 26 52 86 03. Ⓕ Ⓕ
Set in the woods that top the Montagne de Reims this is a showcase for the wines of small growers accompanied by local food. You can also buy Champagne here.

Du Marronnier Ⓡ
7 rue de la Duchesse d'Uzès, 51480 Boursault. Tel 03 26 58 47 52. Ⓕ
This restaurant offers a friendly welcome and simple, wholesome food. The wine list is limited so ask the owner for guidance.

Le Petit Pressoir Ⓡ
2 rue Pasteur, 51480 Boursault. Tel 03 26 58 63 98. Ⓕ Ⓕ
This well-regarded restaurant is owned by a local Champagne grower and serves local food. It is open only at weekends so booking is advisable.

La Porte Oubliée Ⓡ
51700 Châtillon-sur-Marne. Tel 03 26 58 37 58. Ⓕ Ⓕ
Good local cuisine with a touch of innovation.

Le Relais de Reuilly Ⓗ Ⓡ
02850 Reuilly-Sauvigny. Tel 03 23 70 35 36; fax 03 23 70 27 76. Ⓕ Ⓕ
Friendly welcome and beautiful views across the river. The restaurant serves fine, imaginative cuisine and is particularly strong on fish dishes. The wine list has a good and varied selection.

Le Royal Champagne Ⓗ Ⓡ
51160 Champillon. Tel 03 26 52 87 11; fax 03 26 52 89 69. Ⓕ Ⓕ Ⓕ
A Relais & Châteaux hotel with superb views over the Marne Valley. The restaurant serves excellent classic food and has a wine list to match.

L'Union Ⓡ
9 rue de Verdun, 51700 Vincelles. Tel 03 26 51 06 05. Ⓕ
Friendly village restaurant serving simple food.

Wines and Wine Villages

The Marne Valley is generally considered to produce Champagnes that lack the class of those from the Montagne de Reims or the Côte des Blancs. Indeed, the classification of the villages bears this out, for there are no Grands Crus in the valley west of Épernay, and only Hautvillers, Champillon and Cumières are classified as Premier Cru. This is the realm of Pinot Meunier, which constitutes a third of Champagne's planting, and some excellent wines can be found here at reasonable prices.

Boursault (Other Cru 84%, Pinot Meunier) Attractively perched up on the hill and shrouded by woods, Boursault is famous for the impressive neo-Gothic château built by Mme Clicquot in 1845. It is not open to the public, but you can taste the wine made by the present owner.
Best producers: Berat, Ch. de Boursault.

Champillon (Premier Cru 93%, Pinot Meunier) There are wonderful panoramic views over Épernay and the Marne Valley from this small wine village with well-sited, south-facing vineyards. Most of the grapes are used by the local co-operative.

Charly-sur-Marne (Other Cru 80%, Pinot Meunier) A major wine village in the Aisne department, with almost 300ha of vineyards.
Best producers: BARON-ALBERT, BARON-FUENTÉ.

Châtillon-sur-Marne (Other Cru 86%, Pinot Meunier) A large village set back slightly from the river and perched on a hill. Its giant statue of Pope Urban II, who was born here in 1042, is visible from a considerable distance.
Best producer: CHARLIER (at Montigny-sous-Châtillon).

Château-Thierry (Other Cru 80%, Pinot Meunier). Pleasantly situated on both banks of the Marne, this town's main

Champagne attraction is the local co-operative, which makes the Pannier brand.
Best producer: PANNIER.

Cumières (Premier Cru 93%, Pinot Meunier) With its sheltered, south-facing location near the river, this village has been famous for its local red wine since the 14th century.
Best producer: GEOFFROY.

Damery (Other Cru 89%, Pinot Meunier) There are many small growers in this village, whose sole activity seems to be the production of grapes and Champagne.
Best producer: HATON.

Dormans (Other Cru 83%, Pinot Meunier) Small town which contains some interesting churches and a monument commemorating World War One battles on the Marne.

Fleury-la-Rivière (Other Cru 85%, Pinot Meunier) This wine village is worth visiting just

to see the giant frescos on the walls of the local co-opérative, Arnoult.
Best producer: ARNOULT.

Fossoy (Other Cru 80%, Pinot Meunier) Small village set below the main road from Épernay with a 12th-century church.
Best producer: DEHU.

Hautvillers (Premier Cru 93%, Pinot Meunier) This is one of Champagne's most charming villages, and also the best known. Dom Pérignon was the cellarer monk at the former Benedictine abbey, which now belongs to Moët et Chandon and can be visited.
Best producer: Locret-Lachaud.

Oeuilly (Other Cru 84%, Pinot Meunier) This enterprising little village has more to offer than most others in the valley, with its Maison Champenoise and 19th-century schoolhouse.
Best producer: TARLANT.

Reuilly-Sauvigny (Other Cru 80%, Pinot Meunier) This village has only 3ha of vines and all the grapes are sold to Champagne houses.

Villers-sous-Châtillon (Other Cru 86%, Pinot Meunier) Set back from the river in a small valley, this quiet village is full of small growers.
Best producer: CHARPENTIER.

In the Marne Valley vines are planted on the slopes running down to the river. Épernay is in the distance.

On the northern edge of the Côte des Blancs the Romanesque church at Cuis stands above its village and commands a sweeping view of the Montagne de Reims with its heavily forested ridge to the north. The vineyards at Cuis have grown both black and white grapes for well over a century but Chardonnay now accounts for nearly 90 per cent of the plantings. This undulating landscape is typical of the heart of Champagne – the openness of the countryside enables the vineyards on the slopes to enjoy maximum exposure to the sun. The slopes also help keep the vines sufficiently far away from the damp, cold and spring frosts in the deep valleys, provide shelter from extremes of wind and rain and help with crucial drainage.

Looking north from Cuis at the northern end of the Côte des Blancs there are fine views across to the Marne Valley and the slopes of the Montagne de Reims in the distance.

Côte des Blancs

This is the shortest of the four tours in Champagne, but the density of the vineyards and the quality of the wines available mean that there are a large number of excellent producers in this paradise for Chardonnay-based wines.

The Tour

Épernay is not, strictly speaking, a part of the Côte des Blancs – the domination of white grapes starts with the villages of Chouilly and Cuis – but you could well begin the tour by a visit to one of the well-known houses situated on or around the avenue de Champagne. All of them own vineyards in the Côte des Blancs, although for the most part their wines are blended from different grapes and vineyard sources. You will, however, find some Côte des Blancs growers in the town, for example, Gonet-Sulcova.

Leave Épernay by driving down the grand avenue de Champagne, with its splendid 18th- and 19th-century buildings, and following signs for Chouilly, which lies in the middle of the vineyards. If you want to see what a modern Champagne winery is like, visit the producer Nicolas Feuillatte, whose buildings are visible on the hill as you turn up toward Pierry. In fact, the wines are good, even though the building may take some of the magic out of the bubble. Continue to Pierry, where two producers are worth visiting, Henri Mandois Père et Fils, who is a small *négociant*, and Lagache-Gilbert et Fils, a grower.

From Pierry you can see clearly the typical Côte des Blancs landscape: large expanses of vines beginning as soon as the ground starts to slope up toward the flat-topped hills. The slopes become steeper toward the summit, which is covered with clumps of oak. An option here is to continue to Moussy to visit the enterprising producer, José Michel, who is a leading light of the *récoltants-manipulants*. Then, rather than going directly to Cuis, it's worth making a short detour along the D210 to Chavot-Courcourt, where Mont Felix is topped by an isolated 12th-century church lying in a sea of vines, rather like a stranded ship, and the only sign that a whole village once stood here. Skirt around the summit of the hill to the village of Monthelon, and follow this delightful little road through the villages of Mancy and Moslins. Shortly after Moslins, turn right and take the D36 back to the D51, which will return you to the intersection with the D10 road to Cuis, Cramant and Avize, where serious wine-tasting can begin.

At the bottom of the hill in Cuis stands a fine Romanesque church. A signboard makes it easy to find Pierre Gimonnet et Fils, the best-known producer in Cuis,

TOUR SUMMARY

The tour begins at Épernay and continues south through the Côte des Blancs, celebrated for its Chardonnay grapes, as far as Sézanne. This is a peaceful route and there are lovely views over the sweeps of vineyard. The villages are close together and, as well as excellent growers, there are some fine churches.

Distance covered 60km (37 miles).

Time needed 3½ hours.

Terrain These are minor roads but they are easy to drive and well signposted.

Hotels There is a good selection in Épernay and a few more in outlying villages (not necessarily the wine ones) as well as some country inns. There are also some hotels in Sézanne.

Restaurants There is a decent choice for such a small area. Although there are no big stars, there is a good selection of delightful country restaurants.

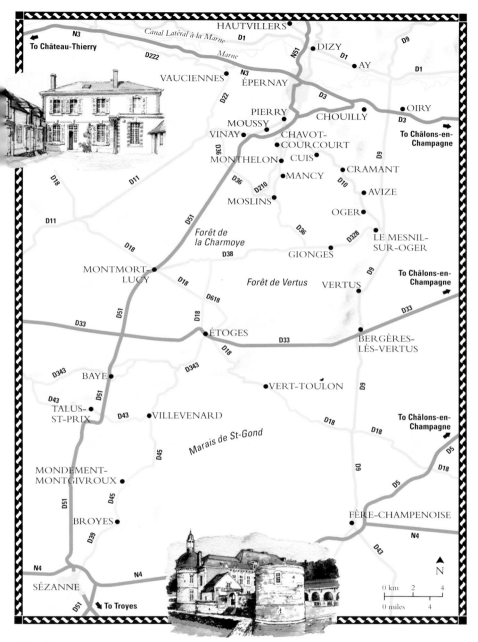

Map illustrations: (above) Delamotte's handsome headquarters in le Mesnil-sur-Oger; (below) Ch. d'Étoges, now a hotel and restaurant.

who also owns vines in Chouilly and Cramant. His wines are archetypal Blancs de Blancs and are highly recommended. As you leave Cuis the countryside is spectacular, with vines sweeping down to the valley floor and the variation in exposure to the sun of the different plots of vines becomes clearly evident.

The entrance to Cramant is marked by a giant bottle, which appears as a sort of doorstop, but it is considerably harder to find the house of Lilbert Fils, which lies to the left of the main road, down a tiny back street just before you reach the church. You can try following the signs that the municipality has thoughtfully put up, with the names of each individual producer, but these have an annoying habit of disappearing just when you need them most. Persevere and don't be afraid to ask your way; showing the name of the producer you are looking for will usually do the trick.

The Lilbert house is tucked away in a narrow street. A tiny courtyard gives onto a crowded room that does triple duty as shipping centre, office and tasting room. This is a small traditional operation with a delightful family touch, and your tasting may well be interrupted by M. Lilbert's small granddaughter wanting to know what's going on.

Lilbert has 4 ha of vineyards, all planted with Chardonnay, which are spread between Cramant, Chouilly and Oiry. The wines are superbly pure in their flavours, and he makes an interesting Champagne of lower pressure, called le Perle, which is delightfully tender. This corresponds to the former Crémant appellation, which the Champenois have abandoned in exchange for other French sparkling wines giving up use of the term *méthode champenoise*. While in Cramant, look out for the shop of the local signmaker, M. Babé. He is responsible for most of the painted wrought-iron signs seen outside growers' houses on the Côte des Blancs, particularly in Avize, the next village south.

Avize is a lively wine village and a good place to buy for a picnic with shops near the main square. It is also full of particularly interesting wines and winemakers, so allow plenty of time here. Maybe the presence of a renowned viticultural school has stimulated the local producers, for there are many excellent ones based in Avize.

If you are curious about the biodynamic approach to agriculture as applied to wine, or just enjoy exceptional Champagnes, then a visit to the producer Jacques Selosse is a must. Now run by Anselme Selosse, who is only the second generation of the family to make wines here, Selosse is near the square in the village centre, marked by one of those wrought-iron signs.

You need to make an appointment to visit, and should not expect plush surroundings, since everything goes into the wine that Selosse makes, including a lot of hard work and enthusiasm. The wines are, unusually, fermented in oak barrels, which vary in age according to the blend being made and even include some new barrels. The usual belief in Champagne is that oak, if it is used at all, should definitely be old so as to avoid giving too strong a taste to the wine and comments were made when Anselme Selosse started using new oak. He has proved that using new oak can be beneficial, provided that the grapes are of good enough quality and that certain procedures are implemented. The

All the best Champagne vineyards are located on chalky slopes. The chalk is able to nourish the vines equally well in both dry and wet years and its brilliant whiteness helps retain both reflect and retain heat. The vineyards at Avize are rated as Grand Cru and are planted entirely with Chardonnay.

wines are well aged, and, unusually, the *dégorgement* date of the Champagne is shown on the labels as additional aging information. These are fabulous wines which will gain extra complexity from further aging.

Back on the square, you can visit de Sousa et Fils, which has another wrought-iron sign in front of the gate. The buildings are attractive and well kept and Erick de Sousa has recently taken over from his father. His Champagnes can be drunk earlier than those of Selosse, since they are softened by undergoing malolactic fermentation.

You may feel like some lunch after all this tasting, so continue south on the D10 to the village of le Mesnil-sur-Oger, where the restaurant, le Mesnil, has a particularly fine wine list. If you want something simpler, turn right on the D328 toward Montmort and up the hill into the woods. There, in the village of Gionges, you will find the Ferme Auberge Nelly Vatel, which uses excellent local ingredients. It is always advisable to book ahead at such places, which are not organized like commercial restaurants. You will also find plenty of places to picnic along this road, which runs through wooded countryside with many ponds, indicating how impermeable the clay soil is on top of the chalk hills.

If you have time and feel like stretching your legs, go as far as Montmort-Lucy, where there is an impressive 16th-century moated château which is open during the summer months or by appointment at other times. There is also a decent hotel and restaurant in Montmort, called the Cheval Blanc. The return trip will take only about 20 minutes, and once back in le Mesnil you can set about the business of visiting a number of top-quality producers who can be found in this, the most famous wine village of the Côte des Blancs and exclusively planted with Chardonnay.

One of the rarest and most expensive of all Champagnes comes from here: Clos du Mesnil, made from grapes from an unusual (for Champagne) walled vineyard by Krug, whose base is in Reims. Another exclusive and rare Champagne from le Mesnil, if slightly more accessible, is Salon, and it is well worth making an appointment to visit this house. Salon makes only Blanc de Blancs, and then only in vintage years, from about 20 separate vineyard lots in le Mesnil. The wines are released for sale only when they have more than 12 years' aging behind them.

Next door to Salon is Delamotte Père et Fils. This is a very old company, founded in the 18th century, but it has remained small. Like Salon, it belongs to Laurent-Perrier. The wines are released onto the market sooner than those of Salon, and are very reasonably priced. Both the vintage and non-vintage Blanc de Blancs are well rounded and mouth-watering. The vintage wine has that lovely nutty taste typical of well-matured, Chardonnay-based Champagnes.

Despite the use of machinery, work in the Champagne vineyards remains very labour-intensive. From May until the harvest, the vines need spraying regularly against pests and disease. These vines are at le Mesnil-sur-Oger, the southernmost Grand Cru village on the Côte des Blancs.

Just across the road from Delamotte is one of le Mesnil's best owner-growers, Guy Charlemagne, and if you walk back toward the village centre, you will see, within its outer walls, the beautiful courtyard and buildings of Pierre Moncuit. White is the dominant colour here, from the chalk of the subsoil and the white Chardonnay grape, to the bright, white-painted reception room where the Moncuits will pour their exquisitely fresh and balanced wines for you. Tasting here is a real delight. The cellars are spectacular, and there is a good collection of older vintages.

Le Mesnil is the last of the Grands Crus on the Côte de Blancs, and Vertus, just to the south, has a lower status in the classification, rating 95 per cent. It is by far the largest of the wine communes of the area and is the first one on this tour where some black grapes are grown, rather than just Chardonnay. This is because of a small pocket of heavier clay soil near Bergères-lès-Vertus. Most of the vineyards face east and they are superbly situated. Vertus' narrow streets with old houses and fountains make this a pleasant one to explore on foot. There are several good restaurants and hotels in Vertus, in particular the Hostellerie de la Reine Blanche. A good small producer to visit is Guy Larmandier, who has vineyards in Vertus, Cramant and Chouilly. The house is in a narrow street that leads up from a tiny square where a statue stands in front of the Café des Arts. You will be shown into a modest, cosy living room to taste delicate, fresh wines with a softish style. This friendly family works as a team, and the daughter, Colette, and her husband produce excellent wines in Cramant under the name of Waris-Larmandier.

The vineyards at Bergères-lès-Vertus mark the southern end of the Côte des Blancs. Down on the plain below the east-facing slopes, wheat takes over from vines as the main agricultural activity.

Southwest of Bergères-lès-Vertus, off the D9, is Mont Aimé, the final hilly outcrop along the Côte des Blancs. Drive up the tiny road to the Table d'Orientation at the top for a final view of the Côte des Blancs stretching northward, South of here vineyards become increasingly rare, and the landscape diversifies into woodland and the St-Gond marshes. The Ch. d'Étoges, a privately owned château that takes paying guests both for dinner and for the night, makes a wonderful place to stay in the area. To reach it, turn right in Bergères-lès-Vertus on to the D33. If you want to taste the Champagne from this area, try Yves Jacques, in the village of Baye, or Nominé-Renard, run by Claude Nominé, in Villevenard. Both villages are south-east of Étoges.

To complete the tour, continue south to the pleasant town of Sézanne which has been an important trading centre since the Middle Ages. The 15th-century church of St-Denis is built on an impressive scale. From the ramparts is a fine view of the peaceful landscape of woods, orchards and vineyards. The wine villages here form the Côte de Sézanne, which extends south almost to Troyes.

Côte des Blancs Fact File

The wine villages of the Côte des Blancs are close together and can be visited easily from Épernay. To the south and east isolated pockets of vineyard continue as far as Sézanne.

Information
Office de Tourisme d'Épernay
See p.25.

Office de Tourisme
Place de la République, 51120 Sézanne. Tel 03 26 80 51 43; fax 03 26 80 54 13.

Musée de la Vigne et du Vin
51190 le Mesnil-sur-Oger. Tel 03 26 57 50 15.

Markets
Sézanne – Wednesday and Saturday mornings

Festivals and Events
Details of annual wine events can be obtained from the Office de Tourisme in Épernay. The Lycée Viticole (wine school) of Avize organizes a fair of wines from all French wine schools on the last weekend in March (tel 03 26 57 79 79).

Where to Buy Wine
Outside Épernay and Sézanne, there are no specialist wine shops. Buy instead from the producers.
La Cave des Lombards
4 rue Bouvier Sassot, 51120 Sézanne. Tel 03 26 42 94 03. Decent choice of Champagnes coupled with reasonable prices.

Where to Stay and Eat
Château d'Étoges Ⓗ Ⓡ
51270 Étoges. Tel 03 26 59 30 08; fax 03 26 59 35 57. Ⓕ Ⓕ This is an ideal combination: a family château in beautiful surroundings that doubles as a hotel. *Cuisine bourgeoise* and a good wine list.

La Croix d'Or Ⓗ Ⓡ
53 rue Notre Dame, 51120 Sézanne. Tel 03 26 80 61 10; fax 03 26 80 65 20. Ⓕ Ⓕ Family-run hotel serving traditional food.

Ferme Auberge Nelly Vatel Ⓡ
Ferme de St-Fergeux, 51130 Gionges. Tel 03 26 57 90 60. Ⓕ Former farmhouse serving food from its own farm produce.

Le Mesnil Ⓡ
2 rue Pasteur, 51190 le Mesnil-sur-Oger. Tel 03 26 57 95 57; fax 03 26 57 78 57. Ⓕ Ⓕ Seasonal dishes and a very impressive wine list.

La Reine Blanche Ⓗ Ⓡ
18 avenue Louis-Lenoir, 51130 Vertus. Tel 03 26 52 20 76; fax 03 26 52 16 59. Ⓕ Ⓕ Friendly hotel and restaurant. Classic cuisine and wine list with unusual choice of older vintages, particularly from Bordeaux.

Wines and Wine Villages

The villages in the Côte des Blancs have more charm and appear less deserted than many of those in the Montagne de Reims or along the Marne Valley.

Avize (Grand Cru, Chardonnay) This delightful, large village is home to the local wine-making school.
Best producers: *Agrapart*, SELOSSE, DE SOUSA.

Baye (Other Cru 85%, Pinot Meunier) Small wine village between Étoges and Sézanne.
Best producer: *Yves Jacques*.

Chouilly (Grand Cru, Chardonnay; Premier Cru 95% black grapes). Village with several interesting buildings.
Best producers: *Nicolas Feuillatte*, *R & L Legras*, *Vazart-Coquart*.

Cramant (Grand Cru, Chardonnay) The wines from here are softer, more forward, than those of Avize or le Mesnil.
Best producers: *Bonnaire*, *Gimonnet-Gonet*, LILBERT, *Waris-Larmandier*.

Cuis (Premier Cru 95%, Chardonnay; Premier Cru 90%, black grapes) Fine Romanesque church and a panoramic view of the Montagne de Reims from the cliff top above the village.
Best producer: GIMONNET.

Étoges (Other Cru 85%, Pinot Meunier) Quiet little village with a 17th-century château open as a hotel and restaurant.

Le Mesnil-sur-Oger (Grand Cru, Chardonnay) Important wine village with an interesting Champagne museum.
Best producers: CHARLEMAGNE, DELAMOTTE, *Launois*, MONCUIT, SALON.

Oger (Grand Cru, Chardonnay) This small village is rather overshadowed by the more famous ones of Avize and le Mesnil and most of the vineyard owners here tend to live elsewhere.
Best producer: *E Bonville*.

Pierry (Premier Cru 90%, Pinot Meunier) Worth exploring to see the 18th-century facades and entrances to the houses.
Best producers: *Lagache-Gilbert*, *Mandois*.

Sézanne (Other Cru 87%, Chardonnay; Other Cru 85%, black grapes) One of the most beautiful and unspoiled towns in the area and worth exploring.

Vertus (Premier Cru 93%, Chardonnay) Bustling town which is home to several medium-sized Champagne houses.
Best producers: LARMANDIER, *Leroy*.

Villevenard (Other Cru 85%, Pinot Meunier) Small village with a Romanesque church.
Best producer: *Nominé-Renard*.

These southern Aube vineyards at Baroville near Bar-sur-Aube are almost on the border with Burgundy. With its beautiful remote valleys, the gently rolling landscape feels quite different to the heart of Champagne around Épernay 110km (70 miles) north. The Aube countryside is quite open with gentle hills and meadows and the vines are confined mainly to the slopes with woods along the ridges. The Aube vineyards are on the same Kimmeridgian soil as Chablis and were finally only included in the official definition of the Champagne vineyard area as recently as 1927.

The Aube

TOUR SUMMARY

A circular tour from Troyes in the southern Aube with its peaceful, rolling countryside, unspoiled villages and vineyards interspersed with wooded hills.

Distance covered 200km (120 miles), including detours

Time needed 7 hours.

Terrain The A5-E54 *autoroute* slices the region in two, so access to the heart of the vineyards is easy. The villages are linked by secondary and minor roads.

Hotels There is plenty of choice in Troyes, but book ahead for hotels in the countryside, since these tend to be small. Bed and breakfast establishments are fairly plentiful.

Restaurants There is a fair selection in the region and many offer local dishes at value-for-money prices.

The city of Troyes, the former capital of the Comtes de Champagne, lies about 90km (56 miles) south of Épernay on the northern edge of the southern Aube vineyards. This is the least-known of Champagne's four main vineyard areas but in many ways it is the most attractive, with vineyards dispersed along a series of slopes around the small towns of Bar-sur-Aube and Bar-sur-Seine. In this area of mixed farming, making Champagne is by no means the only activity, but the Aube Champagnes need not be shy of comparison with their more prestigious, northern cousins.

The Tour

Begin or end your tour with half a day spent in Troyes; with its half-timbered houses and narrow pedestrian streets, it is an interesting city to explore. If you want to taste some Champagnes without going too far, you can try those from Montgueux, immediately west of Troyes, but the main Aube vineyards are spread out around the towns of Bar-sur-Aube and Bar-sur-Seine. It is easier to start with the region

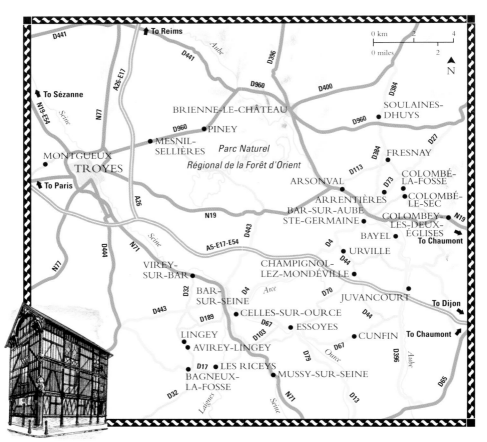

near Bar-sur-Aube, so leave Troyes and head east on the A5 *autoroute*. You start to see vineyards on the left about half way between the first two *autoroute* exits. After about 50km (30 miles), take the second exit (No. 25) and follow the signs to Abbaye de Clairvaux.

If you are interested in glass-making, continue on the road toward Bar-sur-Aube for about 12km (7½ miles) to Bayel, where the 300-year-old Cristalleries Royales de Champagne still uses traditional blowing techniques to make some of the best Champagne glasses available. Otherwise, turn left at Clairvaux on the D12 to the Abbey, which was an important religious institution but is now a prison, although parts of the old abbey can be visited on Saturdays.

After passing through an oak and beech forest, the road emerges into open countryside, with vineyards on the slopes to the right and the *autoroute* to the left, and at the entrance to the village of Champignol-lez-Mondéville, you will see the sign for R Dumont et Fils. A new house, perched on a small mound to the left, is the home and winery of the Dumont family, who have a spotlessly clean and well-organized set-up. Their Champagne can be tasted in a delightfully light and airy room which looks out over the vineyards. The wines are noticeably softer and warmer in feel than those of the Côte des Blancs, for example, with clean, gentle fruit flavours and good definition.

In the village, turn right toward Bar-sur-Aube, picking up the D44, the *route touristique du Champagne*, and follow signs to the small village of Urville and the Champagne house of Drappier. Over the brow of the hill, the vista opens out onto vineyards and a series of small valleys. Based in an impeccably restored and enlarged old building, Drappier has some magnificent 12th-century cellars. The family moved to Urville from Reims in the 19th century and their name, which means clothier, reveals their original profession, one which they share with many of the most illustrious houses, since Champagne used to be the cloth-trading centre of France. André Drappier produces an informative newsletter and a wide range of well-made Champagnes, including some older vintages and an unusual Extra-Dry. You can simply turn up to taste, but make an appointment if you want to visit the cellars.

From Urville, make your way to Bar-sur-Aube via the D4. This town has emerged relatively unscathed from the destruction of successive wars, and the medieval layout is virtually intact. There are some lovely old houses in the town, and an unusual covered market place called Halloy, which surrounds the church. The first town here, in Celtic and then Roman times, was perched on the nearby hill of Ste-Germaine, and it is well worth driving up there for a magnificent view of the surrounding countryside. This

Bar-sur-Aube is a peaceful town with some attractive medieval wooden houses.

Map illustration: a Renaissance house in Bar-sur-Seine.

means going back down the D4 for 3km (2 miles), then taking a narrow road to the left that leads to the chapel of Ste-Germaine. A nearby farm produces excellent goat's milk cheese, so bring the other ingredients for a picnic.

To explore the Bar Auboise, head north-east on the D73 to Arrentières, where the wines of Denis Chaput are particularly recommended, as are those of Philippe Cudel in Colombé-la-Fosse. Colombé-le-Sec has a remarkable 12th-century vaulted granary which belonged to Clairvaux Abbey. If you want to see all the villages called Colombé, or Colombey, there are two good reasons for heading east to Colombey-les-deux-Églises. One is that this was the home of General de Gaulle, who is buried here. The other is to have lunch at the Auberge Montagne, which is small and old-fashioned with good food. It also has a few bedrooms.

This little diversion will take you to the eastern limit of the Champagne vineyards. To visit the Bar-sur-Seine area, find your way back to Bayel via the N19; then, heading south on the D396, pass under the *autoroute* and turn right to Cunfin and Essoyes. The vineyards, which reappear to the right of the road, announce the start of the Bar-sur-Seine area. Essoyes is another place of pilgrimage, this time for lovers of Impressionist painting, since this is where Renoir lived. It also has a wine museum, the Maison de la Vigne, where you can taste the local Champagnes.

Les Riceys has its own AC for a dark, golden pink, still wine called Rosé des Riceys. It is relatively expensive as not very much is made and then only in the ripest years.

From Essoyes, various minor roads lead south-west to the beautiful villages of Ricey-Haut, Ricey Haute-Rive, and Ricey-Bas, known together as les Riceys. The villages run confusingly into one another, and specific parts of the vineyards around them produce small quantities of Champagne's rarest wine, Rosé des Riceys, a still wine from Pinot Noir. Pascal Morel, in Ricey-Haut, is most welcoming and makes superb wines. His Rosé des Riceys is made only in vintage years and spends a year in barrels before bottling, so preserving vibrantly fresh fruit flavours; with age, the wine takes on the aromas of red Burgundy. Morel's Champagnes, also dominated by Pinot Noir, are rich and full flavoured, with excellent aging capacity.

Now go west to Bagneux-la-Fosse, then north on the D32. Between Avirey-Lingey and Lingey, on your left you will see the neat-looking courtyard and buildings of Champagne Serge Mathieu. This family estate makes some beautifully fragrant Champagnes which are properly aged before being sold. You can visit the cellars and taste wines in a well-organized tasting room where English is spoken.

On the way to Bar-sur-Seine, you can turn off the N71 to Celles-sur-Ource to visit Emmanuel Tassin, a family-run Champagne business. Finish your tour in Bar-sur-Seine, with its half-timbered houses and a fine restaurant, le Parc de Villeneuve, just south of the town by the river.

The Aube Fact File

A visit to the Aube vineyards can easily be combined with one to the bustling city of Troyes where the old quarter contains many fine half-timbered houses.

Information

Comité du Tourisme de l'Aube
34 quai Dampierre, 10096
Troyes. Tel 03 25 42 50 91;
03 25 42 50 88.

Office de Tourisme de Troyes
16 boulevard Carnot, 10000
Troyes. Tel 03 25 73 00 36;
fax 03 25 73 06 81.

Maison de la Vigne
Essoyes. Tel 03 25 29 60 47.
Small wine museum.

Markets

Troyes – daily in les Halles,
every morning

Festivals and Events

The *Fête de St-Vincent* is held on
22 January in most villages.

Where to Buy Wine

Les Caves de la Cité
7 rue Cité, 10000 Troyes. Tel 03
25 80 58 15.

Cellier St-Pierre
1 place St-Pierre, 10000 Troyes.
Tel 03 25 80 59 25.

La Pinardière
25 avenue du Général Léclerc,
10200 Bar-sur-Aube. Tel 03 25
27 28 04.

Where to Stay and Eat

Le Chanoine Gourmand ®
32 rue de la Cité, 10000 Troyes.
Tel 03 25 80 42 06; fax 03 25 80
92 00. Ⓕ Ⓕ
Next to the cathedral, with
excellent food, especially fish.

La Chaumière ®
N19, 10200 Arsonval. Tel 03 25
27 91 02; fax 03 25 27 90 26. Ⓕ
Old-style auberge with a shady
terrace. The owner is English.

La Clef des Champs ®
10220 Mesnil-Sellières. Tel 03
25 80 65 62. Ⓕ
Excellent country restaurant.

Auberge Montagne Ⓗ ®
52330 Colombey-les-deux-
Églises. Tel 03 25 01 51 69;
fax 03 25 01 53 20. Ⓕ Ⓕ
Small, old-fashioned hotel
serving traditional country food.

Le Parc de Villeneuve ®
Hameau de Villeneuve, N7,
10110 Bar-sur-Seine. Tel 03 25
29 16 80; fax 03 25 29 16 79.
Ⓕ Ⓕ Ⓕ
Superb house in a park
overlooking the river, just south
of the town. Top-quality classic
food and a well-chosen wine list.

Hotel de la Poste Ⓗ ®
35 rue Émile Zola, 10000
Troyes. Tel 03 25 73 05 05;
fax 03 25 73 80 76. Ⓕ Ⓕ
Modernized old building serving
good food. The wine list has fine
old Burgundy and Bordeaux
wines at unbeatable prices.

Le Relais Saint-Jean Ⓗ
51 rue Paillot-de-Montabert,
10000 Troyes. Tel 03 25 73 89
90; fax 03 25 73 88 60. Ⓕ Ⓕ
Renaissance building with
spacious, well-furnished rooms.

Wines and Wine Villages

All the Aube wine villages are classified at 80% on the Champagne growth scale, except for Villenauxe-la-Grande. Pinot Noir is the main grape in the Aube.

Arrentières (Pinot Noir) The remains of an old château can be seen in the village.
Best producer: Chaput.

Avirey-Lingey (Pinot Noir) Actually two small villages, of which Avirey is the larger, at the western extremity of the Aube vineyards.
Best producer: SERGE MATHIEU.

Bar-sur-Aube This is the largest town within the Aube Champagne-producing area, but curiously it has no producers. Prosperous in the Middle Ages, as its attractive architecture shows, it is on the right bank of the Aube river and surrounded by wooded hills.

Bar-sur-Seine This was a wealthy commercial town during the Renaissance period. It is now home to the largest Aube Champagne producer, the Union Auboise co-operative, which uses several brand names, including Vve A Devaux, and is well-organized for visits.
Best producer: VVE A DEVAUX.

Champignol-lez-Mondéville (Pinot Noir) There is a 12th-century chapel at Mondéville.
Best producer: DUMONT.

Colombé-la-Fosse (Pinot Noir) The village has a church dating from the 12th and 16th centuries.
Best producer: Cudel.

Colombé-le-Sec Full of architectural and archaeological interest. Production is handled mainly by a co-operative.

Essoyes (Pinot Noir) Famous as the painter Renoir's home. There is also a wine museum.

Montgueux (Chardonnay) West of Troyes and separated from the Aube vineyards.
Best producers: DOUÉ, *Lasseigne-Berlot, Therret.*

Les Riceys (Pinot Noir) Famous for the production of the rare still Rosé des Riceys.
Best producers: Defrance, de Forez, MOREL.

Urville (Pinot Noir) Charming village and home to the only sizable Aube Champagne house.
Best producer: DRAPPIER.

The three ruined castles set in the foothills of the Vosges high above the village of Ribeauvillé serve as a reminder that for more than a thousand years Alsace has been a border province and bitterly fought over in successive wars. These medieval castles were originally inhabited by the powerful Counts of Ribeaupierre who owned Ribeauvillé. The well-preserved castle of St-Ulrich is the largest and most beautiful of the three, with a 13th-century keep and knights' hall. The Minstrels' Festival, or Pfifferdai, held every September in Ribeauvillé, celebrates the time when minstrels would come to pay homage to the count. It is worth walking up from Ribeauvillé through the vineyards to the castles for stunning views over the Alsace countryside.

Hunawihr's fortified church is one of the best-known landmarks along the wine route in Alsace.

Touring Alsace

The landscape of Alsace is noticeably different from that of most other parts of France. This is due partly to the Germanic influence, which is particularly noticeable in the architecture, and partly to the fact that in this much fought-over region buildings are seldom found isolated in the countryside, but are grouped together in a network of well-preserved villages. Although the cities of Strasbourg and Colmar contain many masterpieces of urban architecture, it is these prosperous wine villages, and their insertion into the landscape, that give Alsace its unique atmosphere.

Alsace's vineyards are strung out in a narrow band of land on the eastern foothills of the Vosges, running north to south for 120km (75 miles) from Marlenheim, west of Strasbourg, to Thann, west of Mulhouse. The vineyards are sandwiched between the Vosges mountains in the west and the A35 Strasbourg to Mulhouse *autoroute* down on the Rhine plain in the east. The better vineyards cling to the slopes or the higher ground, which provide drainage and increased exposure to the sun, as well as reduced yields. The wine villages are linked by a series of minor roads, some of which constitute a well-signposted *route du vin*. It is very easy to meander through the vineyards, or to take the *autoroute* and travel quickly between Strasbourg and Colmar, in the heart of the vineyards, to visit a particular destination. The two tours divide the vineyards into a northern section, from Strasbourg to Colmar, essentially within the Bas-Rhin department, and a southern section from Colmar to Thann, in the Haut-Rhin.

Accommodation is plentiful in Alsace, with hotels at most price levels. These range from *chambres d'hôte*, or bed and breakfast, to comfortable 4-star hotels in Strasbourg, and some luxury hotels in the countryside. Alsace attracts considerable tourism from neighbouring Germany and Switzerland, and the European Parliament sits at Strasbourg, so it is advisable to book ahead at most times of the year.

Avoid harvest time if you hope to be welcomed with open arms by the winemakers. This generally takes place between mid-September and mid-October, apart from late harvesting which, weather permitting, will spread out at a leisurely pace until November; but things are generally calm again by mid-October. In August half the population of France can be on the roads, including some of the winemakers. So the best time to visit is undoubtedly from April to June, when the vines are growing fast, and then again just after the harvest, when the vine leaves turn to gold, and you may be able to hear or see tanks of wine under fermentation in the cellars.

SUMMARY OF TOURS

Northern Alsace Running from Marlenheim, one of the oldest wine villages in Alsace, south to Colmar, Alsace's wine capital, this tour covers the stretch of vineyards within the Bas-Rhin department. The wine route twists and turns along the foothills of the Vosges and most of the villages are only a few kilometres apart.

Southern Alsace The Haut-Rhin department starts just north of Colmar, and the wine route continues south to Thann, due west of Mulhouse. The scenery is more impressive on the whole on this tour as the Vosges mountains are higher and more rugged. Vineyards become less intensive at the southern end and the wine villages are more spread out.

Strasbourg

The capital of Alsace is a delightful city to visit on foot as all the major sights are in the centre on an island in the river Ill. In the old quarter called Petite France, the narrow streets are built around a series of canals. The 13th-century cathedral has magnificent old stained glass and there are some fine museums with famous collections.

Strasbourg Fact File

The richness of the city's wine and food culture lies chiefly in the *winstube*, inexpensive wine taverns which serve local dishes and wines in a convivial atmosphere. They are all within walking distance of the cathedral.

Strasbourg's old city is on an island formed by two branches of the river Ill. Many of the narrow medieval streets here are pedestrianized.

Information

Office Départemental du Tourisme du Bas-Rhin
17 place de la Cathédrale, 67082 Strasbourg. Tel 03 88 52 28 28; fax 03 88 52 28 29. Hotel reservations: tel 03 88 52 28 22 or 03 88 32 51 49.

Palais de Rohan
2 place du Château, 67000 Strasbourg. Tel 03 88 52 50 04. Houses 3 of Strasbourg's major museums, including the interesting Musée Archéologique, which contains evidence that the Romans cultivated vines in Alsace.

Musée Alsacien
23 quai St-Nicolas, 67000 Strasbourg. Tel 03 88 52 50 04. The museum includes a section on wines and wine-making.

Markets

Marché Broglie – Wednesday and Friday
Marché du quai Turckheim – Wednesday and Friday mornings
Marché des Rohans – Saturday morning

Festivals and Events

So many festivals and events take place in Strasbourg that it is impossible to cover them here. It's best to obtain a list from the Office de Tourisme and a copy of *Strasbourg Actualités*.

Where to Buy Wine

These wine shops sell a wide range of Alsace wines.

L'Art du Vin
16 rue d'Austerlitz, 67000 Strasbourg. Tel 03 88 35 12 28. A fine range from all over France and a good selection of Alsace wines. Very helpful.

La Sommelière
1 rue Fossé-des-Tailleurs, 67000 Strasbourg. Tel 03 88 32 78 59. Wines from some of Alsace's best producers. Also sells *foie gras*.

Where to Eat

Here is a small selection of the many restaurants in the city.

Le Buerehiesel Ⓡ
4 parc de l'Orangerie. Tel 03 88 61 62 24; fax 03 88 61 32 00. Ⓕ Ⓕ Ⓕ
The most inventive cuisine in Alsace and well-chosen wines.

Le Clou Ⓡ
3 rue du Chaudron. Tel 03 88 32 11 67; fax 03 88 75 72 83. Ⓕ
One of the best traditional *winstube*. Copious portions and a friendly atmosphere. You'll need to book ahead here.

Le Crocodile Ⓡ
10 rue de l'Outre. Tel 03 88 32 13 02; fax 03 88 75 72 01. Ⓕ Ⓕ Ⓕ
Classic 3-star Michelin restaurant. Fine food, excellent service and a great wine list at reasonable prices.

Au Gourmet sans Chiqué Ⓡ
15 rue Ste-Barbe. Tel 03 88 32 04 07; fax 03 88 22 42 40. Ⓕ Ⓕ
Light, inventive food and good Alsace wines.

Julien Ⓡ
22 quai des Bateliers. Tel 03 88 36 01 54; fax 03 88 35 40 14. Ⓕ Ⓕ Ⓕ
Cosy, elegant dining room, with a view across the river Ill. Modern, inventive Alsace food.

Maison Kammerzell Ⓡ
16 place de la Cathédrale. Tel 03 88 32 42 14; fax 03 88 23 03 92. Ⓕ Ⓕ Ⓕ
Wonderful medieval building; some dining rooms are frescoed and have a view of the cathedral. Good, varied menu and decent wine list.

Au Pont-Corbeau Ⓡ
2 quai St-Nicolas. Tel 03 88 35 60 68; fax 03 88 35 60 68. Ⓕ Ⓕ
Excellent place to taste the best of *winstub*-type traditional Alsace cooking. Good wine selection.

Le Saint-Sepulcre Ⓡ
15 rue des Orfèvres. Tel 03 88 32 39 97. Ⓕ
Probably the most authentic of Strasbourg's many *winstube*.

Steckelburger Ⓡ
8 rue des Tonneliers. Tel 03 88 32 76 33. Ⓕ
Small, unpretentious, with good fresh food and decent wines.

Sternstebele Ⓡ
17 rue des Tonneliers. Tel 03 88 21 01 01; fax 03 88 21 01 02. Ⓕ Ⓕ
Modern, well-decorated friendly *winstub*, more like a wine bar, near the cathedral. Good food.

*High above the medieval village of
Riquewihr is the south-facing
Schoenenbourg Grand Cru vineyard.*

*Map illustrations: (above) old house
in Obernai; (below) St-Sébastien
chapel outside Dambach.*

TOUR SUMMARY

The tour covers the northern
section of the Alsace wine route
which is mainly in the Bas Rhin
department. The vineyards start
at Marlenheim south of
Strasbourg and the tour
continues as far as Colmar.

Distance covered   100km
(62 miles) or more, excluding
detours.

Time needed   This tour can
easily fill 1–2 days or more, since
there is so much to see and taste
along the wine route.

Terrain   Away from Strasbourg
the route winds along
departmental roads and smaller
country roads that can be slow-
moving but are easy to follow. In
summer, the wine route can
become very crowded.

Where to stay   Strasbourg has a
wide range of hotels and there
are some good ones in the larger
wine villages and in Colmar.

Where to eat   There are plenty
of simple *winstube* with
inexpensive menus, as well as
several very good restaurants
serving excellent food.

Northern Alsace

The vineyards of Alsace run north to south, with a slight westward drift, in an almost uninterrupted strip some 120km (75 miles) long. For convenience this tour concentrates on the section north of Colmar.

The Tour

It is not easy to find your way out of Strasbourg, so tortuous is the one-way system, and so dense the network of *autoroutes* that encircles the city. Follow the blue signs, first toward Nancy and Metz, and then Saverne. Do not take the *autoroute*, but find the N4, which is the old road to Paris that runs west toward the Vosges mountains. After the village of Ittenheim, vineyards become visible on the hillsides ahead and from time to time you can see the long poles of hop fields (Alsace produces over 50% of France's beer). After about 16km (10 miles), just before Marlenheim, on the righthand side, there is a fairly simple information centre on the *route du vin* (the wine route). Marlenheim is worth a brief visit for its 18th-century houses, and for a meal or a night at le Cerf, one of Alsace's best restaurants, which is rated two stars by Michelin.

The *route du vin* has its northern entry point at Marlenheim, although there are some isolated pockets of vineyards further north. To start the trail, turn left off the N4 just after Marlenheim, by a sawmill. A small detour to the right takes you to Wangen, a charming little village with narrow streets and cobbled squares huddled behind its 13th-century walls; the church has some fine, 15th-century stained glass windows. The road runs back to the D142, which leads to Westhoffen through rolling countryside with mixed farming, while the vineyards cling to the higher ground. Westhoffen is famous for its cherries, and the orchards are much in evidence. You have to keep alert in its winding streets to find the left turn to the D625 to Traenheim.

In the village of Traenheim, turn left toward Scharrachbergheim and Molsheim and follow the winding main street (called rue Principale) to the winery of Frédéric Mochel, a particularly friendly grower. Like so many in Alsace, his winery surrounds an impeccably kept courtyard, with an old wine press in a corner. The wine Mochel likes to be judged by is the Riesling Cuvée Henriette, from the Grand Cru Altenberg de Bergbieten. It is clear as a bell, with a rich, flowery nose rarely found in a Riesling, and a very clean palate-feel. Almost delicate on first impression, Mochel's wines have surprising power and will age very well.

From Traenheim pick up the D422 toward Molsheim. It is worth stopping in Avolsheim, the next village after

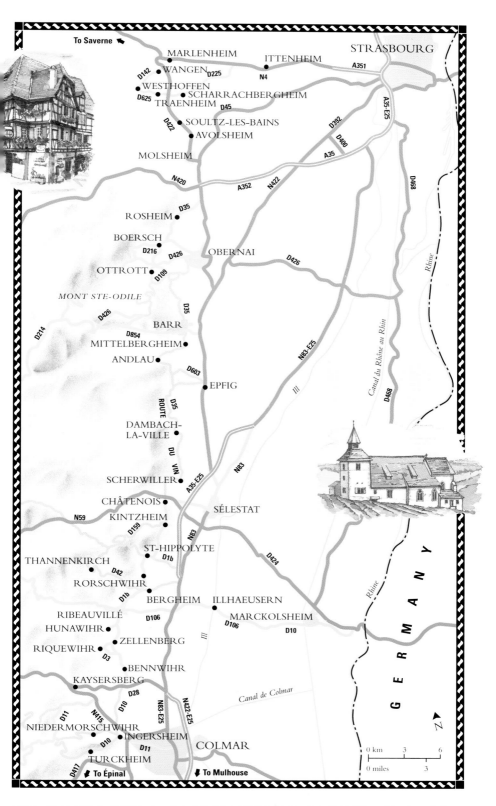

To Saverne

MARLENHEIM
ITTENHEIM
STRASBOURG
D142
WANGEN
D225
N4
A351
WESTHOFFEN
D625
SCHARRACHBERGHEIM
TRAENHEIM
D45
A35-E25
D422
SOULTZ-LES-BAINS
D392
AVOLSHEIM
D400
MOLSHEIM
A35
N420
A352
N422
D468

ROSHEIM
D35

BOERSCH
D216
D426
OBERNAI
D426

OTTROTT
D109

MONT STE-ODILE

D426
D35

BARR
D854
MITTELBERGHEIM
ANDLAU
D603
EPFIG
Ill

D214

ROUTE
D35
DAMBACH-
LA-VILLE

DU

SCHERWILLER
VIN
A35-E25
N83
N83-E25

Canal du Rhône au Rhin
D468

Rhine

CHÂTENOIS
KINTZHEIM
N59
D159
SÉLESTAT
N83

ST-HIPPOLYTE
THANNENKIRCH
D1b
D42
D424
RORSCHWIHR
D1b
BERGHEIM
ILLHAEUSERN
RIBEAUVILLÉ
D106
MARCKOLSHEIM
HUNAWIHR
D106
D10
RIQUEWIHR
ZELLENBERG
Ill
D3
BENNWIHR
KAYSERSBERG
D10
D28
Canal de Colmar
N83-E25
N422-E25

D11
N415
NIEDERMORSCHWIHR
D10
INGERSHEIM
D11
COLMAR
D417
TURCKHEIM
To Épinal
To Mulhouse

GERMANY

Rhine

N

0 km   3   6
0 miles   3

Soultz-les-Bains, to take a look at an early Romanesque baptistry, and an even older, although heavily rebuilt, church, the Dompeter. This is possibly the oldest church in Alsace, since it dates back to the 6th century. It is now in the middle of fields and has a deserted, although well-kept, feel.

Molsheim is an attractive small town, full of architectural and other treasures. Just down the street that leads into the town centre, at 49 route de Saverne, is the cellar of Bernard Weber, an attentive grower, whose wines come from a small 6-ha holding, half of which is on the Grand Cru Bruderthal. Riesling is his speciality, and his wines are among the freshest and cleanest in Alsace: the cutting edge of Alsatian wines, deliberately dry, and very refreshing. All show sharp fruit flavours, with an angular austerity that resembles the man himself: enthusiastic, but restrained. The opulent Vendanges Tardives are made only in very ripe years, which seldom occur here, since Molsheim is in the slightly cooler, northern part of Alsace and he believes that they must happen naturally (1989 was the last for him).

Around Molsheim's beautiful place de l'Hôtel de Ville, which features the extraordinary Renaissance Metzig, or Butchers' Hall, you will find all kinds of useful shops. The most important for wine lovers is l'Ami Sommelier, which not only can provide you with a fine selection of wines from 40 Alsace producers, but can also provide many items for a decent picnic. The town also has its claim to automobile fame as the home of Bugatti cars. There is a small Bugatti museum here, but if you are car-crazy, wait until you reach Mulhouse, at the southern end of the wine trail, where you will find the biggest motor museum in France.

Out of Molsheim, make for Obernai on the D422, but shortly turn right on to the D35 to Rosheim. You are now heading toward the mountains and Mont Ste-Odile, which plays an important role in local mythology. Rosheim has an unusually long and straight (for Alsace) main street, bridged by no fewer than three tower gateways, and a fine Romanesque church whose origins date back to the 11th century, although it has been burned to the ground a few times since.

Stay on the D35 (this is going to become a familiar phrase) through Boersch and then turn right, uphill, to Ottrott, which is one of Alsace's rare red-wine producing areas. In the upper village, there are several welcoming hotels, at all prices, and just as many restaurants, since Ottrott is a base for the walkers who set off into the mountains behind to work up an appetite for the mammoth portions of *choucroute* and other hearty fare that awaits them back in the friendly village inns.

Ottrott itself is not of great interest, but it is a convenient place in which to stay. When wandering around, do not

Obernai is one of the oldest towns in Alsace and is famous for its connection with Ste Odile, the region's 7th-century patron saint, who was born here. There is a statue of the saint on top of the fountain in the beautiful market square.

miss a squat little 12th-century church, totally hidden away between the upper and lower villages. The most notable buildings at Ottrott are the two ruined castles above the village, which are within easy walking distance. Before leaving, go to the lower village and try Jean-Charles Vonville's red wines, especially the Réserve Rouge d'Ottrott, as decent reds are hard to come by in Alsace.

From Ottrott, you can opt for a bit of sightseeing and shopping in Obernai, or continue on the wine route. To reach Obernai, simply continue downhill on the D426. It is the prototype of the picture-postcard small Alsace town, with half-timbered houses, a fairy-tale bell tower, and a surfeit of trinket shops. Nevertheless, it contains some fine buildings, grouped around the splendid Renaissance town hall and its square. Some streets are pedestrianized, which makes shopping easier. If you get hungry or thirsty, there are hotels and restaurants of all description here.

The next stop south is Barr, which contains an interesting museum of local furniture in a house called la Folie Marco. Park in or near the fine village square. On the way to the museum, which lies a short distance back along the D35, stop to taste the wines of Pierre Hering, who makes complex, crisp wines that are admirable examples of the dry Alsace style. His son speaks good English and will show you around the traditional cellar.

Heading south from Barr, the road climbs through vineyards to the tiny village of Mittelbergheim. This is a good place for a break if you need one after all the tasting. The Hôtel et Winstub Gilg is not, despite what it says, a *winstub*, but an attractive classic restaurant, with a few pleasant rooms. Across the road, Armand Gilg, a cousin, will be happy to let you taste his wines.

Down the hill is Andlau, set in a valley with the steep slopes of the Kastelberg vineyard on the right. Andlau has some fine Renaissance and 17th-century houses and a remarkable Romanesque church, whose entrance should not be missed. Park next to the church, and you will find the shop and winery of Marc Kreydenweiss just across the road. The shop is full of bottles from all over the world, which demonstrates the owner's curiosity about all wines. Kreydenweiss's vineyard techniques follow biodynamic principles, which excludes the use of chemical sprays. His wines are very pure, with strong personalities, and usually require several years of bottle-aging to reveal their full potential; the labels on the bottles are works of art in themselves. Mme Kreydenweiss speaks good English.

If unusual wines with personality and a creative spirit behind them are your interest, then continue to Epfig, where André Ostertag has his winery. He is one of the most innovative winemakers in Alsace, and an appointment here can

Records show that Mittelbergheim has had vineyards since 388. It is a beautifully preserved wine village and Sylvaner is the local speciality.

Access to the fortified village of Bergheim is still through the half-timbered, 14th-century tower gateway or Porte Haute.

be a rewarding experience. His wines are beautifully balanced and put the emphasis on pleasure and delicacy, rather than sheer power. He is also a poet and his tasting room houses works of art.

Return to the wine route and drive south to Dambach-la-Ville, a medieval town that has retained the greater part of its 14th-century walls and gateways. Around lies quintessential Alsace landscape, with vineyards climbing over the hills and villages perched on the slopes. Dambach has one of the largest vineyard areas of any wine commune in Alsace, and in the 18th century a quarter of its population made their living from barrel-making. There are still plenty of excellent growers here today, such as Arnold, Clog and Gisselbrecht. The D35 road takes you out of the village to Scherwiller, and toward the ruins of Ch. d'Ortenbourg, visible on the skyline. An option here is to take a short drive down to Sélestat, to visit the town centre, where there is a remarkable medieval library and some other fine buildings. It can also be a useful place to find a hotel if the smaller ones on the *route du vin* are full.

Back on the wine route, above the village of Kintzheim, just south of Châtenois, is the Ch. de Haut-Koenigsbourg, one of the rare medieval castles in Alsace not in ruins. It was restored early this century by the German Kaiser Wilhelm II, and is well worth visiting. The road up to it through the beautiful beech and larch forests is spectacular, as is the view from the château, which is now a medieval museum. This is the perfect place from which to observe the relief of the Alsace vineyards, running down from the Vosges mountains to the Rhine plain.

An option from here is to take the back road to Bergheim, via Thannenkirch, where there is one of the most delightful auberges in Alsace, la Meunière, with an excellent restaurant.

The next village on the wine route, Ste-Hippolyte, is soon followed by Rorschwihr, where, hidden away behind the church, are the premises of the Rolly Gassmann family. Here you will receive the warmest of welcomes. Tasting in the fairly dark cellar can be a memorable experience, since the Gassmanns make a wide range of wines, mostly lusciously fruity and soft, and tend to insist on your tasting them all. Make sure you find the spittoon before you start, or bring someone else to drive you.

Bergheim is a sizeable but relatively quiet village with a magnificent tower gateway dating from 1300. Just outside the gateway, on the road leading to Ribeauvillé, are the premises of Marcel Deiss. The company is run with great enthusiasm by Jean-Michel and Clarisse Deiss. Jean-Michel is one of the most vociferous defenders of the virtues of low yields from specific Grand Cru vineyards, and his wines are precise in their flavours and built to last. If you want to experience how Riesling can vary from one vineyard to another, this is the place to do it.

Bergheim is an ideal place in which to stop for some wine-tasting and also refreshment, for, as well as Deiss, Gustave Lorentz and Domaine Spielmann are also excellent producers. The Winstub du Sommelier, with the best wine list in the area, is just beyond the gateway. Chez Norbert, a little further down the street, is an enjoyable place to stay and also has an excellent wine list.

A few kilometres south, down the D1b, is Ribeauvillé, one of Alsace's prime tourist attractions. Just before entering the village, on the righthand side, in a building crowned by a strange half-timbered tower, is F E Trimbach, one of the best-known producers in Alsace. Like that of many Alsace wine-making families, the story of the Trimbachs goes back several hundred years. Their best-known wines are the Rieslings, especially the long-lived Clos Ste-Hune and Cuvée Frédéric-Émile; indeed, all their wines are reliable.

In summer it is best to leave the car outside Ribeauvillé as parking is extremely difficult. If you are driving into the village to a hotel, and there are several here including the very good inn, les Seigneurs de Ribeaupierre, check its location first, since it is almost impossible to stop in the narrow streets. The main street is called Grand Rue, and a walk along its cobbled way will give you a fair picture of what an Alsace town might have been like in the 17th century. The *winstub* Pfifferhüs is very good but quite small, so booking is advisable.

From Ribeauvillé, the last lap of this route leads to Colmar, Alsace's wine capital, via the villages of Hunawihr,

Two of Ribeauvillé's best Grand Cru vineyards, Geisberg and Kirchberg, overlook the village on a perfectly sited, south-facing slope.

Zellenberg and Riquewihr. Hunawihr lies a little way off the D1b, but it is a particularly attractive village, with a fortified graveyard and some 15th-century frescos in the church tower. A walk in the surrounding vineyards (all the wine villages have well signposted paths through the vines) will give you an excellent idea of the way Alsace villages integrate with the landscape.

From Hunawihr, return to the D1b and head toward Colmar. You can take the first road to your left for a visit to the small village of Zellenberg, which, unusually for Alsace, is perched on the crest of a hill rather than down in the valley. Here, just past the church, are the cellars of a young producer called Marc Tempé. He has just started making his own wine, although he has many years of experience in advising others, and, if the quality of his first vintages (1995 and 1996) are anything to go by, Tempé is definitely a name to watch.

Last stop on this tour is Riquewihr, which necessitates a sharp right turn immediately after Zellenberg. Riquewihr is the perfect 17th-century wine village, ringed with vineyards and with hardly anything out of place along its picturesque, narrow, cobbled main street. Like Ribeauvillé, it can become a bottleneck for traffic in the height of summer, when busloads of tourists descend on it, but out of high season it's definitely worth a visit.

Hugel is Riquewihr's leading wine-making family and this wrought-iron sign made by the famous Alsace artist, Hansi, advertises its wine shop in the main street.

At the entrance to the village are two of Alsace's biggest wine companies: Dopff et Irion and Dopff au Moulin. The latter has been a prime instrument behind the successful growth of Alsace's sparkling wine, Crémant d'Alsace. Halfway up the main street is the shop of another great Alsace name, Hugel et Fils. This family-owned company has pioneered the fabulous Vendanges Tardives, or late-harvest wines, in Alsace and also maintains the rare and laudable policy of selling its wines only when they are ready for drinking. If you make an appointment, you will be taken round the cellars and given a tasting by a member of the Hugel family, but if you do not want to make a lengthy visit just show up at the shop and taste wines there.

The road into Colmar runs down through Bennwihr and will take just a few minutes. Colmar is in the heart of Alsace's wine country, roughly halfway along the *route du vin*. Its extensive pedestrian area and wonderful collection of old houses, many lying along a canal in the area known as la Petite Venise, give the town a very special attraction. It can easily be explored in half a day, since the old quarter is compact and must be visited on foot. There are car parks all around the area, so you should not have to walk too far. Colmar is full of good restaurants and hotels at all price levels, so is an ideal place in which to break your journey before starting on the next tour of southern Alsace.

Northern Alsace Fact File

Colmar is almost exactly at the north-south centre of the vineyards, and at the southern end of this tour. It contains few winemakers but is very much the wine capital of Alsace and makes a useful starting or finishing point for any tour.

Information

Conseil Interprofessionnel des Vins d'Alsace (CIVA) (Maison des Vins d'Alsace)
12 avenue de la Foire-aux-vins, 68012 Colmar. Tel 03 89 20 16 20; fax 03 89 20 16 30.
Very helpful. Information and an interesting and interactive display on Alsace wine today.

Office Départemental du Tourisme du Bas-Rhin
See p.49.

Association Départementale du Tourisme du Haut-Rhin
1 rue Schlumberger, 68006 Colmar. Tel 03 89 20 10 68; fax 03 89 20 10 68.
General tourist information, and booklets on restaurants and all types of accommodation.

Musée d'Unterlinden
1 rue d'Unterlinden, 68000 Colmar. Tel 03 89 20 15 50; fax 03 89 11 26 22.
Diverse, high-quality collection, including Grünewald's Issenheim altarpiece. There is also a section on early wine-making.

Markets

Weekly markets are held in all the major villages. They are always in the mornings and occasionally continue after 12am.

Festivals and Events

On 1 May there is a *Foire aux vins* in Molsheim; in Riquewihr the *Foire aux vins* is combined with a marathon race on the 3rd Sunday in May. July is a busy month: there is a *Nuit du vin* in Dambach-la-Ville on the 1st Saturday; a *Fête du vin* in Barr on the 2nd weekend, a *Foire aux vins* on the 3rd weekend in Ribeauvillé, and one in Mittelbergheim on the last weekend, when there is also a *Fête de l'Ami Fritz* in Hunawihr. On the 1st weekend in August, a

Fête du vin takes place in Andlau and a *Fête du Gewurztraminer* in Barr. In September, the Minstrels' Festival or *Pfifferdai* takes place in Ribeauvillé on the 1st Sunday, Riquewihr has a *Fête du vin* every weekend, and Bergheim a *Fête du vin nouveau* on the last weekend. A *Fête des vendanges* is held in Bergheim on the 1st weekend in October and on the 2nd weekend there is a *Fête du vin nouveau* in Mittelbergheim and a *Fête du raisin* in Molsheim.

Where to Buy Wine

There are wine shops in Colmar and in some villages. All the producers mentioned in the Wine Villages section (see p.59) welcome cellar-door sales.

L'Ami Sommelier
1 place de l'Hôtel de Ville, Molsheim. Tel 03 88 38 20 20.
Excellent selection of wines plus local dishes and other food.

Maison Pfister
11 rue des Marchands, 68000 Colmar. Tel 03 89 41 33 61.
Good selection of wines in the most beautiful house in Colmar.

La Sommelière
Place de la Cathédrale, 68000 Colmar. Tel 03 89 41 20 38.
The best wine shop in Colmar, with an excellent selection.

Where to Stay and Eat

Abbaye de la Pommeraie Ⓗ Ⓡ
8 avenue du Maréchal Foch, 67600 Sélestat. Tel 03 88 92 07 84; fax 03 88 92 08 71. Ⓕ Ⓕ Ⓕ
A luxurious hotel, with 2 restaurants and a fine wine list.

Auberge des Alliés Ⓗ Ⓡ
39 rue des Chevaliers, 67600 Sélestat. Tel 03 88 92 09 34; fax 03 88 92 12 88. Ⓕ
Right in the old city centre, with simple bedrooms full of

charm; the décor of one of the dining rooms dates back 300 years. Good traditional food.

L'Ami Fritz Ⓗ Ⓡ
8 rue des Châteaux, 67530 Ottrott-le-Haut. Tel 03 88 95 80 81; fax 03 88 95 84 85. Ⓕ Ⓕ
This perfect cosy Alsace auberge serves excellent food and wine. Some of the bedrooms are in an annexe.

Beau Site Ⓗ Ⓡ
Place de l'Église, 67530 Ottrott-le-Haut. Tel 03 88 95 80 61; fax 03 88 95 86 41. Ⓕ Ⓕ
Modernized, within a traditional Alsace house, and in the centre of the village.

Au Boeuf Rouge Ⓡ
6 rue du Docteur Stolz, 67140 Andlau. Tel 03 88 08 96 26; fax 03 88 08 99 29. Ⓕ Ⓕ
Old auberge serving both traditional Alsace and classic cuisine, along with local wines.

Le Bugatti Ⓗ
Rue de la Commanderie, 67120 Molsheim. Tel 03 88 49 89 00; fax 03 88 38 36 00. Ⓕ
Comfortable, cheaper annexe of Hôtel Diana (see p.58).

Burenwinstubel Ⓡ
15 rue de la Monnaie, 67120 Molsheim. Tel 03 88 38 14 84. Ⓕ
Great place for *flammekeuche*, or *tarte flambée*. The wine list includes the owner's own wines.

Le Cerf Ⓗ Ⓡ
30 rue de Général de Gaulle, 67520 Marlenheim. Tel 03 88 87 73 73; fax 03 88 87 68 08. Ⓕ Ⓕ Ⓕ
Family-run hotel which has one of Alsace's best restaurants, serving typical, yet up-to-date food. Superb wine list.

Chez Norbert Ⓗ Ⓡ
9 Grand-Rue, 68750 Bergheim. Tel 03 89 73 31 15; fax 03 89 73 60 65. Ⓕ Ⓕ
Medieval building surrounding a courtyard with a few pleasant bedrooms. Good restaurant with a great wine list.

Le Clos des Délices (H) (R)
17 route de Klingenthal, 67530
Ottrott. Tel 03 88 95 81 00;
fax 03 88 95 97 71. (F) (F) (F)
On the edge of the forest, with
all the trappings of luxury.
Modern French cuisine.

Le Clos St-Vincent (H) (R)
Route de Bergheim, 68150
Ribeauvillé. Tel 03 89 73 67 65;
fax 03 89 73 32 20. (F) (F)
Beautifully situated hotel with
panoramic view over vineyards.
Classic cuisine.

Hôtel le Colombier (H)
7 rue Turenne, 68000 Colmar.
Tel 03 89 23 96 00; fax 03 89 23
97 27. (F) (F) (F)
Elegant conversion of lovely old
houses in the Petite Venise area.

La Cour d'Alsace (H) (R)
3 rue de Gail, 67210 Obernai.
Tel 03 88 95 07 00; fax 03 88 95
19 21. (F) (F)
Refined hotel located around a
courtyard. Classy restaurant and
also a *winstub*.

Hôtel Diana (H) (R)
14 rue Ste-Odile, 67120
Molsheim. Tel 03 88 38 51 59;
fax 03 88 38 87 11. (F) (F)
Luxurious hotel with sauna and
swimming pool. Good food and
excellent wine.

Le Fer Rouge (R)
52 Grand Rue, 68000 Colmar.
Tel 03 89 41 37 24; fax 03 89 23
82 24. (F) (F) (F)
Wonderfully inventive, modern
cuisine with an Alsace touch.
Fine but expensive wine list.

Hôtel et Winstub Gilg (H) (R)
1 route du Vin, 67140
Mittelbergheim. Tel 03 88 08 91
37; fax 03 88 08 45 17. (F) (F)
Friendly, cosy hotel offering
classic food.

Le Haut-Ribeaupierre (R)
1 route de Bergheim, 68150
Ribeauvillé. Tel 03 89 73 62 64;
fax 03 89 73 36 61. (F) (F) (F)
Light, modern cuisine.

Auberge de l'Ill (R) /**Hôtel des
Berges** (H)
Rue de Collonges-au-Mont-d'Or,

68970 Illhaeusern. Tel 03 89 71 83
23; fax 03 89 71 82 83. (F) (F) (F)
This is one of the best restaurants
in France and in a glorious
situation on the banks of the
river Ill, surrounded by gardens.
The hotel is in an annexe.

La Metzig (R)
Place de l'Hôtel de Ville, 67120
Molsheim. Tel 03 88 38 26 24. (F)
Brasserie food served in
magnificent surroundings.

Auberge la Meunière (H) (R)
68590 Thannenkirch. Tel 03 89
73 10 47; fax 03 89 73 12 31.
(F) (F)
Up in the hills with a view of
Ch. de Haut-Koenigsbourg, this
small auberge has a fine restaurant.

Le Petit Bouchon (R)
11 rue de l'Ours, 68000 Colmar.
Tel 03 89 23 45 57. (F) (F)
Excellent food, more Lyonnais
than Alsatian. Decent wine list.

Pfifferhüs (R)
14 Grand-Rue, 68150
Ribeauvillé. Tel 03 89 73 62 28;
fax 03 89 73 80 34. (F) (F)
The perfect *winstub* in a fine old
building. Friendly welcome,
with good food and a small
selection of excellent wines.

Au Raisin d'Or (H) (R)
28 bis rue Clemenceau, 67650
Dambach-la-Ville. Tel 03 88 92
48 66; fax 03 88 92 61 42. (F) (F)
Welcoming rooms and good
honest food.

S'Rappschwirer Stebala (R)
6 place de l'Ancien-Hôpital,
68150 Ribeauvillé. Tel 03 89 73
64 04. (F)
Good *winstub*-cum-brasserie.

Le Relais de la Poste (R)
1 rue des Forgerons, 67140
Andlau. Tel 03 88 08 95 91. (F)
Good *winstub* with a modern
touch to the cuisine. Excellent
wines at reasonable prices.

Caveau St-Pierre (R)
24 rue de la Herse, Petite Venise,
68000 Colmar. Tel 03 89 41 99
33; fax 03 89 23 94 33. (F)
Good substantial local food, and
a view over the canal.

Le Sarment d'Or (H) (R)
4 rue du Cerf, 68340 Riquewihr.
Tel 03 89 47 92 85; fax 03 89 47
99 23. (F) (F)
Pleasant rooms in a 16th-century
house. Modern Alsace cuisine and
very good wine list.

Schillinger (R)
16 rue Stanislas, 68000 Colmar.
Tel 03 89 41 43 17; fax 03 24 28
87. (F) (F) (F)
Superb classic, modern cuisine
and a good wine list.

Auberge du Schoenenbourg (R)
2 place de la Piscine, 68340
Riquewihr. Tel 03 89 47 92 28;
fax 03 89 47 89 84. (F) (F) (F)
Overlooks the village ramparts
and vineyards. Classic, modern
cuisine and wines by the glass.

**Les Seigneurs de
Ribeaupierre** (H)
11 rue du Château, 68150
Ribeauvillé. Tel 03 89 73 70 31;
fax 03 89 73 71 21. (F)
Friendly, cosy hotel off the main
street serving good breakfasts.

Winstub du Sommelier (R)
51 Grand-Rue, 68750 Bergheim.
Tel: 03 89 73 69 99. (F) (F)
Excellent food and superb wines,
many available by the glass.

Au Tire Bouchon (R)
29 rue du Général de Gaulle,
68340 Riquewihr. Tel 03 89 47
91 61; fax 03 89 47 99 39. (F)
Winstub in a converted barn
serving simple, local food.

La Tour (H) (R)
1 rue de la Mairie, 68150
Ribeauvillé. Tel 03 89 73 72 73;
fax 03 89 73 38 74. (F) (F)
Modern hotel with comfortable
rooms and *winstub* in an old
house in the town centre.

Le Vignoble (H)
1 rue de l'Église, 67650 Dambach-
la-Ville. Tel 03 88 92 43 75. (F)
Small, charming and inexpensive.

Zinck Hôtel (H)
13 rue de la Marne, 67140
Andlau. Tel 03 88 08 27 30;
fax 03 88 08 42 50. (F)
A converted mill, with each room
decorated in a different style.

Wines and Wine Villages

Alsace's lovely wine villages nestle among the vineyards in the Vosges foothills. The wine route between the villages is well signposted.

Andlau   (Grands Crus: Kastelberg, Moenchberg, Wiebelsberg) Andlau grew up around the large Romanesque abbey church founded in 880 by Richarde, the wife of Emperor Charlemagne. This, and the elegant houses, show how prosperous the town used to be. There are two ruined castles on the hills above the town.
Best producers: *Durrmann, Gresser,* KREYDENWEISS, *Wach.*

Barr   (Grand Cru: Kirchberg de Barr) Fine old hillside town with an interesting museum in the 18th-century villa called the Folie Marco.
Best producers: HERING, *Stoeffler, Willm.*

Bergheim   (Grands Crus: Altenberg de Bergheim, Kanzlerberg) Riesling and Gewurztraminer both do well here. The village is pleasant and not too crowded in the summer.
Best producers: DEISS, LORENTZ, SPIELMANN.

Colmar   This bustling town of immense charm is the centre of the local wine trade and hosts a major wine fair in August. There are some good wine shops, too.
Best producer: SCHOFFIT.

Dambach-la-Ville   (Grand Cru: Frankstein) The village is surrounded by 15th-century walls with watchtowers and medieval gateways.
Best producers: ARNOLD, *Beck-Hartweg, Clog, Gisselbrecht, J Haufler, Ruhlmann-Dirringer.*

Epfig   Although Epfig has no Grand Cru and little architectural charm, one of Alsace's best winemakers lives here.
Best producer: OSTERTAG.

Hunawihr   (Grand Cru: Rosacker) The imposing church with its fortified graveyard and

The village of Bergheim is full of beautifully restored, brightly painted, half-timbered houses.

15th- and 16th-century frescos, is a well-known sight along the *route du vin*. A stork centre and butterfly park are other points of interest. Famous for its Riesling, particularly that from the exceptional Clos Ste-Hune vineyard, within the Rosacker Grand Cru, which belongs to F E Trimbach.
Best producers: *Hunawihr co-operative, Mittnacht.*

Mittelbergheim   (Grand Cru: Zotzenberg) The vineyards date back to the 4th century and are particularly noted for Sylvaner.
Best producers: *Boeckel,* GILG, *Rietsch, Seltz.*

Molsheim   (Grand Cru: Bruderthal) A 14th-century gateway remains one of the ways into Molsheim. The magnificent Renaissance Metzig, or Butcher's Hall, is situated in the town square; the ground floor is now a *winstub*.
Best producers: *Klingenfus, Neumayer,* WEBER.

Ottrott   Nestling at the foot of Alsace's holy Mont Ste-Odile, with its 7th-century surrounding wall and chapel, Ottrott is a good centre for walking. It is one of the few villages in Alsace which is noted for red wine.
Best producer: *Vonville.*

Ribeauvillé   (Grands Crus: Geisberg, Kirchberg and Osterberg) One of Alsace's tourist attractions, Ribeauvillé has many beautiful 17th-century houses and 2 fine Gothic churches. Its vineyards have a very good reputation for Gewurztraminer and Riesling. On *Pfifferdai*, the annual feast day in September, the streets are full of strolling musicians. Walk up through the vineyards and forest to visit the ruined castles of Girsberg, Haut-Ribeaupierre and St-Ulrich and for wonderful views over the countryside.
Best producers: KIENTZLER, *Ribeauvillé co-operative, Jean Sipp, Louis Sipp,* F E TRIMBACH.

Riquewihr   (Grands Crus: Schoenenbourg and Sporen) Arguably the most beautiful village in Alsace and a major centre of the wine trade. It's worth looking at the village from the hills behind, since you will get a rare view of the overall aspect and layout of a medieval village that has grown without being radically altered.

It is delightful to wander around the pedestrianized centre of the village, where there are good shops and places to eat. A small museum is dedicated to Hansi, a famous local artist and signpainter.
Best producers: DOPFF ET IRION, DOPFF AU MOULIN, HUGEL, *Lehmann, Mittnacht-Klack.*

Rorschwihr   There are no Grands Crus around this small village, but some excellent wines come from specific vineyards, or *lieux-dits*.
Best producer: ROLLY GASSMANN.

Traenheim   This unassuming wine village is the mythical home of the Teutonic heroes of the epic poem, the *Niebulengenlied*.
Best producer: MOCHEL.

Zellenberg   (Grand Cru: Froehn) A pretty, peaceful small village and unusual in Alsace for being built on top of a hill.
Best producers: *Becker,* TEMPÉ.

Pinot Gris is often used to make Sélection de Grains Nobles wines as its skin is more susceptible to rot, including the beneficial noble rot, or *Botrytis cinerea*, than that of any of the three other Alsace 'noble' varieties. These vines, in the Steinert Grand Cru at Pfaffenheim, were left unpicked at the time of the main harvest so that the botrytis fungus could develop on the grapes. Alsace's hot November sunshine is crucial to this development which will gradually shrivel the grapes and concentrate the sugar. This can take anything from several days to several weeks and as the grapes shrivel and sweeten it is vital to protect them from the local bird population. In Alsace botrytis occurs only haphazardly and so consecutive sweeps, or *tries*, have to be made through the vineyard to pick just the botrytized grapes. Any bunches that have not been sufficiently botrytized are used for Vendange Tardive wines that are less concentrated.

A former monastery, the Clos des Capucins, is now the home of the Faller family who run Domaine Weinbach.

Map illustrations: (above) half-timbered houses in Colmar; (centre) typical Alsace wrought-iron sign in Guebwiller; (below) the centre of Turckheim.

Southern Alsace

The wine villages to the west of Colmar are so numerous that you need to zigzag constantly if you want to visit them all. South of Guebwiller the vineyards start to thin out, and there is a gap before you reach the southern gateway of the *route du vin* at Thann.

The Tour

Take the D10 road from Colmar toward Strasbourg, which will take you past the airport and give you the opportunity to stop at the Maison des Vins d'Alsace. This is the home of the official wine body in Alsace, the Conseil Interprofessionnel des Vins d'Alsace (CIVA), which can provide maps and other information in several languages. There is also an interesting display on how Alsace wines are made, and even what some of them smell like.

Soon after leaving the CIVA, turn left on the D1b toward Kientzheim and Kaysersberg. Alsace's wine museum is housed in the château at Kientzheim; this will give you a full picture of the history and present-day techniques involved in making wines in Alsace. Also in Kientzheim, near the church, is the producer, Paul Blanck, whose wines are excellent.

Kaysersberg is famous as the birthplace of Dr Albert Schweitzer, the philosopher and founder of the mission at Lambarene in the Congo. It is a magnificent small town, with brightly coloured houses, many with Renaissance sculptures on their facades. Wander through its streets for an hour or so and there are excellent food shops.

An unforgettable experience is a visit to the Domaine Weinbach, the property of Mme Faller and her two daughters, Laurence and Cathérine. It is situated on the left just before Kaysersberg, and can be recognized easily by the wall that circumscribes the Clos des Capucins, a former monastery which is now the Faller home and winery. The vineyard within the Clos (which means 'walled enclosure') is very fine. Here, if you take the trouble to make an appointment, you will be received in the living room and taste wines which are among the most delicate and deliciously fruity in Alsace. Pure pleasure.

From Kaysersberg, take the *route du vin* toward Ingersheim, then turn right to Niedermorschwihr. In this village, perched in the vineyards, is one of the most extraordinary jam-makers in France, Christine Ferber, who works from the family *pâtisserie*. Her range is true to the Alsace tradition of 'if it grows, it must be edible'. The road on to Turckheim, twisting through the vineyards, is delightful. Coming over the crest of the hill, look out for the sign

TOUR SUMMARY

This route is a little shorter than the northern one, and depending on the number of stops you make, it is feasible to visit Colmar in the morning, and finish at Thann at the end of the day.

Distance covered 80km (50 miles).

Time needed 3½ hours, excluding detours.

Terrain The route meanders through the wine villages, but the driving is easy except in summer when the roads can be very crowded.

Hotels Although there are a few good options in the countryside, Colmar has a greater choice of hotels.

Restaurants There is a fair selection of places at which to eat. The recommended restaurants offer regional dishes at value-for-money prices.

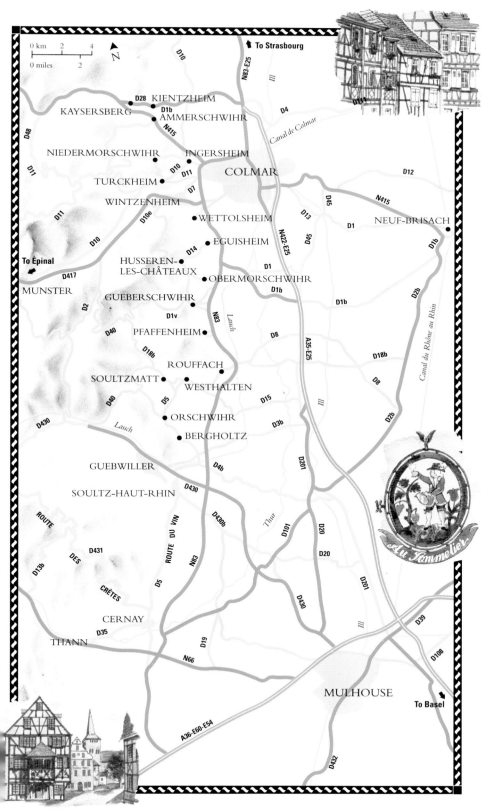

0 km   2   4

0 miles   2

N

To Strasbourg

N83-E25

D10

D28 KIENTZHEIM

KAYSERSBERG
D1b
AMMERSCHWIHR

D4

Canal de Colmar

N415

NIEDERMORSCHWIHR   INGERSHEIM

D10   D11

COLMAR

D12

D10e

TURCKHEIM
D7

WINTZENHEIM

D45

N415

D11

D10e

WETTOLSHEIM

D13   D45

D1

NEUF-BRISACH

D11

D10

D14

EGUISHEIM

N422-E25

D45

D1b

To Épinal

HUSSEREN-
LES-CHÂTEAUX

D1

D417

OBERMORSCHWIHR

D1b

D2b

MUNSTER

D2

GUEBERSCHWIHR

D1b

Canal du Rhône au Rhin

D1v

N83

Lauch

D40

PFAFFENHEIM

D8

A35-E25

D18b

D18b

D2b

ROUFFACH

D8

SOULTZMATT

WESTHALTEN

D40   D5

D15

D2b

Lauch

ORSCHWIHR

D3b

D201

BERGHOLTZ

D4b

GUEBWILLER

D430

SOULTZ-HAUT-RHIN

D430b

Thur

D101

D20

ROUTE

D431

D430b

N83

D20

DES

D138

ROUTE DU VIN

D201

CRÊTES

D5

D430

D39

CERNAY

D35

D19

D108

THANN

N66

MULHOUSE

To Basel

A36-E60-E54

D432

63

marking the famous Grand Cru vineyard of Brand, where Pinot Gris does particularly well. From up here there is a wonderful view of the village, with its coloured roofs and church spire. You will probably be able to pick out the nest of a stork (Alsace's emblem) perched on top of the spire.

Bordered by a stream, Turckheim is a very attractive village with a distinctly medieval feel to it. Finding a restaurant on a Wednesday can be a problem, since it is closing day, but the marvellous old inn, the Hôtel des Deux Clés, is open then and offers a warm welcome. The undisputed star of Turckheim's winemakers is the Domaine Zind-Humbrecht whose distinctively modern new cellar is on the road to Colmar. The wines are excellent and very concentrated in their flavours, but, sadly, often out of stock. You will need an appointment to visit.

Wintzenheim is on the main D417 road that leads to Munster, well known for its cheese, and on to Épinal. Since the cheese is widely available, there is no particular point in driving up the valley to visit Munster, unless you have plenty of time, although the first part of the valley is pretty and you can see clearly how the vines cling to the hillsides. In Wintzenheim, on the main road opposite the Cristal Hôtel, you will find the property of a well-known winemaker called Josmeyer. The large, colourful courtyard is impressive, and the wines here are particularly enjoyable.

Head toward Colmar and, on coming out of the village, take a right turn to Wettolsheim. Unlike some Alsace villages, this is much more a working village than a tourist attraction, and some very good winemakers are based here. The road just by the church leads to the property of Barmès-Buecher, which is the last building on the right before you reach the vineyards. The young owners make excellent wines, and they are very friendly but, as usual with small growers, it is advisable to make an appointment, since they may be in their vineyards.

Eguisheim, built in three concentric circles around a small château, is next on the route. Dating back to the 13th century, its narrow streets are worth exploring on foot and you can follow a series of signs. At the entrance to the town stands the Eguisheim co-operative, which uses the brand name Wolfberger for its wines. It is well organized for tastings and visits of all types.

In the centre, next to the château, is the shop of Léon Beyer, one of the great figures of Alsace wines. Main streets in Alsace are almost always called Grand Rue, and the one in Eguisheim is no exception. Walk along the Grand Rue until you reach place Charles de Gaulle, where, at number 8, you will find the house and cellars belonging to Paul Ginglinger, an affable man with a charming, friendly wife. They have modernized their traditional buildings in a most

These Riesling vines belong to Zind-Humbrecht, the leading producer of wines from the famous Brand Grand Cru, a large, steep, south-facing vineyard above Turckheim.

successful blend of old and new, and it is a pleasure to sample wines in the well-lit tasting room, which has a fascinating family tree on the wall illustrating how deep-rooted wine-making traditions are in Alsace. Ginglinger's wines are of a pure, lightly minerally style, smooth but never soft.

A visit to Eguisheim would not be complete without trying one of its excellent restaurants. Particularly recommended is le Caveau d'Eguisheim in the place du Château. It has two restaurants at different price levels and superb food. The owners also run a delightful hotel, the Hostellerie du Château, across the street. If you're buying for a picnic, all you need can be found close to this square.

If you want a break from the *route du vin*, head east across country for 15km (9 miles), or via Colmar, to the town of Neuf-Brisach with its famous octagonal fortress. It has retained the austere aspect of Vauban's 17th-century fortified town, which was destined to defend Alsace for the French monarchy. A visit to Neuf-Brisach is also a good excuse to have lunch in a delicious little restaurant, la Petite Palette, run by a talented and modest young chef.

South-west, and uphill, from Eguisheim on the D14, lies Husseren-les-Châteaux, the highest point of Alsace's vineyards, dominated by the ruins of the châteaux of Eguisheim. This is the starting point of a fine two-hour walk known as the *route des cinque châteaux*, even though there are only three visible ruins today. As you drive out of the village, the Kuentz-Bas winery soon appears on the right and you need to make a sharp right turn into the gateway. This friendly, family-owned company makes excellent wines, mainly in a full and aromatic style.

Three ruined châteaux, the Tours d'Eguisheim, dominate the skyline above Husseren-les-Châteaux. Up in the Vosges foothills, the vineyards here are the highest in Alsace.

If you make an appointment, Christian Bas, whose English is excellent, will give you a guided tour, but no appointment is needed to sample the wines in the homely, *winstub*-like tasting room with its terrace overlooking the valley. There is a small wine museum and Kuentz-Bas also produces a useful little guidebook to restaurants in France, which is available on request.

From here, head south on the D1 to Obermorschwihr, and on to Gueberschwihr, which is a very fine village with an alpine feel to it; mercifully it is by-passed by tourist hordes. Sandstone, which underlies the surrounding vineyards, notably the Grand Cru Goldert, is the chief building material here, and the pink sandstone Romanesque bell tower dominates the village. Wine-making traditions go back at least to the 8th century in this beautiful village, which contains some of Alsace's most magnificent large houses dating from the 16th and 17th centuries, as well as several old gateways and fountains.

Park in the village square, near the rather massive and extensively rebuilt church, then walk up the narrow street to the left of the town hall. Soon a magnificent wrought-iron sign indicates Maison Ernest Burn. It is well worth making an appointment here to taste the superb wines, which are the equal of the fine surroundings – the courtyard, the house with its carved doorway and spiral stone staircase and the splendid cellars. Burn's top wines are from the Clos St-Imer vineyard, which lies within the Goldert Grand Cru; the Tokay-Pinot Gris, Gewurztraminer and Muscat all have great finesse and are full of deep fruit, yet never overpowering. Indeed, the entire range, including the more basic wines, is good.

Back down in the valley, Pfaffenheim may not seem to have a lot going for it, but the co-operative is conveniently situated on the outskirts of the village, near the N83. The factory-like building is no beauty, but you can turn up without an appointment. It is also well organized, with helpful staff and a qualified *sommelier* who will unravel the intricacies of Alsace's wines. There is a huge range of well-made wines, including very fine Pinot Gris. You may also find some older vintages that are otherwise hard to come by.

The next village south is Rouffach, with an imposing church, which covers the transition between Romanesque and Gothic architecture, and interesting Renaissance buildings around the huge village square. To reach it head toward Soultzmatt on the N83, then turn off on to the D18b; don't miss the modern buildings belonging to René Muré just after the junction. He owns the particularly well-sited, terraced vineyard of Clos St-Landelin, located within the Vorbourg Grand Cru, and which you can admire from the tasting room overlooking the valley, known as la Vallée Noble, which leads to Soultzmatt. With such a view, it is easy to meditate on the influence of the slope and the sun's angle on the ripening of grapes. In fact, Muré is able to make a very good red wine from this vineyard, showing what Pinot Noir can do, though it rarely does in Alsace, as well as intense Riesling and Tokay-Pinot Gris. His other wines give an impression of restrained and refined power.

A little way up the valley is Soultzmatt, which is so well protected by the surrounding hills that Mediterranean plants flourish here. Gewurztraminer does well here. The magnificent Grand Cru Zinnkoepflé with its hot, dry mesoclimate has its prime ambassador in the person of Seppi Landmann, who can be found in the centre of Soultzmatt. Another good winemaker, who produces an excellent sparkling Crémant d'Alsace, is Léon Boesch. Just before Soultzmatt, take the D5 to Orschwihr, which celebrates a Crémant d'Alsace festival on the first weekend in July.

Once in Orschwihr, follow the signs to Domaine Lucien Albrecht, just down the Grand Rue on the left. Neat as a pin, the courtyard and buildings have been renovated by

The St Wolfgang chapel stands at the foot of the Pfingstberg Grand Cru, outside the village of Orschwihr.

Jean Albrecht, who runs the property with his wife Michèle. The domaine dates back to 1772, and visitors are welcomed to a well-lit tasting room which dates back to the same period. Magnificent Vendange Tardive wines are among the specialities here, as are fine Rieslings and Pinot Gris from the Grand Cru Pfingstberg.

A little further down the D5, in the village of Bergholtz, is the home of Jean-Pierre and Marthe Dirler, who make some particularly fine wines from the three Grands Crus – Saering, Kessler and Spiegel – in which they have vineyards. The Dirlers produce Riesling, Pinot Gris, Muscat and Gewurztraminer from these vineyards, as well as an interesting range of wines from the rest of their property. The beautiful wood panelling of their tasting room makes a magnificent backdrop to such well-made wines.

The last wine town before the vineyards start to thin out toward Thann, is Guebwiller on the river Lauch at the foot of the Florival, a pretty valley leading up into the Vosges. As you drive through the village, look out for signs to Domaines Schlumberger, the biggest single domaine in Alsace with 140ha of vines – about three-quarters of Guebwiller's vineyards. The vineyards are on an extremely steep slope and are largely terraced, and there is a greater concentration of Grands Crus here than anywhere else in Alsace.

Guebwiller is a town with some industrial activity, but the long history and high reputation of its wines have generated wealth and, therefore, over a long period, buildings of considerable architectural interest, including the Romanesque church and 16th-century Hôtel de Ville.

Finally, take the road to Thann to see the spectacularly steep vineyards above the town. Rangen, which is the name of Thann's Grand Cru, is certainly the steepest vineyard in Alsace and possibly in France. Although its celebrity goes back to the 12th century, the difficulty of working such a vineyard had led to its being almost abandoned until the early 1970s. But due in particular to the determination of Léonard Humbrecht of Domaine Zind-Humbrecht, its terraced slopes are once again fully productive, although Rangen's two best growers do not live in Thann – Zind-Humbrecht is based in Turckheim and Schoffit in Colmar. Rangen's poor, stony soil is unique in Alsace because it contains volcanic rock, and the flavours of the top Rangen wines have something of an explosive nature. Historically famous for Tokay-Pinot Gris, it is now well known for exciting Riesling and Gewurztraminer as well.

Thann also contains an impressive Gothic church, the Collégiale St-Thiébaut, one of the most beautiful in Alsace and with a fine collection of medieval sculpture. This is the most southerly point of the *route du vin*, and from here the road continues to Mulhouse only 15km (9 miles) away.

The town of Thann lies far below the Clos St-Urbain vineyard on the hill of Rangen. The steeply terraced, south-east facing vineyard, famous for its Riesling, is owned by Zind-Humbrecht.

Southern Alsace Fact File

The Alsace vineyards form an almost continuous north-south strip, but it is convenient to consider Colmar or the border between Bas-Rhin and Haut-Rhin as a midway point. The climate is warmer in the south and the vineyards become more scattered after Guebwiller.

Information

Conseil Interprofessionnel des Vins d'Alsace (CIVA) (Maison des Vins d'Alsace)
See p.57.

Association Départementale du Tourisme du Haut-Rhin
See p.57.

Musée du Vignoble et des Vins d'Alsace
1 Grande Rue, 68240 Kientzheim. Tel 03 89 78 21 36. The Ch. de Kientzheim is home to a wine museum and also the Alsace wine fraternity, the Confrérie St-Étienne.

Markets

Thann – Saturday morning

Festivals and Events

In May near Ascension Day Rouffach holds a *Foire du vin biologique*. There are several festivals in July: the *Fête du Crémant* at Orschwihr on the 1st Saturday; the *Nuits des Grands Crus* on the 3rd Friday at Eguisheim; the *Fête des Guinguettes d'Europe* on the 3rd weekend at Husseren-les-Châteaux; and the *Fête du vin* at Wettolsheim on the last weekend. On the 1st weekend in August, Turckheim has its *Fête du vin* and Soultzmatt its *Nuits des Grands Crus*. There is a *Fête de l'amitié* at Gueberschwihr on the 3rd weekend of August and a *Fête des vignerons* at Eguisheim on the 4th weekend. Wintzenheim has a *Fête d'automne* on the 1st weekend of October, and Kientzheim a Foire St-Martin on the 1st weekend in November.

Where to Buy Wine

There are some excellent wine shops in Colmar (see p.57) and in some of the villages. All the producers on p.69 welcome cellar-door sales.

Where to Stay and Eat

L'Ange Ⓗ Ⓡ
125 rue des Trois Épis, 68230 Niedermorschwihr. Tel 03 89 27 05 73; fax 03 89 27 01 44. Ⓕ Traditional inn in the centre of the village.

Chambard Ⓗ Ⓡ
9–13 rue du Général de Gaulle, 68240 Kaysersberg. Tel 03 89 47 10 17; fax 03 89 47 35 03. Ⓕ Ⓕ Ⓕ
This elegant restaurant serves fine, classic cuisine accompanied by wonderful wines. The hotel with comfortable bedrooms is in a modern annexe.

Hostellerie du Château Ⓗ
2 place du Château, 68420 Eguisheim. Tel 03 89 23 72 00; fax 03 89 23 68 80. Ⓕ Ⓕ
Delightful modern conversion of an old house in the town centre.

Château d'Issenbourg Ⓗ Ⓡ
68250 Rouffach. Tel 03 89 78 58 50; fax 03 89 78 53 70. Ⓕ Ⓕ Ⓕ
A Relais & Châteaux hotel with park and swimming pool overlooking the vineyards and the Rhine Valley. Excellent cuisine and a very interesting wine list which has 1000 wines from all over France and also from a few other countries.

Hôtel Constantin Ⓗ
10 rue du Père Kohlmann, 68240 Kaysersberg. Tel 03 89 47 19 90; fax 03 89 47 37 82. Ⓕ
Attractive small hotel in a converted old house.

Hôtel des Deux Clés Ⓗ Ⓡ
68230 Turckheim. Tel 03 89 27 06 01; fax 03 89 27 18 07. Ⓕ
Lovely old-fashioned hotel.

Caveau d'Eguisheim Ⓡ
3 place du Château, 68420 Eguisheim. Tel 03 89 41 08 89; fax 03 89 23 79 99. Ⓕ Ⓕ

The restaurant serves excellent, inventive cuisine and local wines. There is a *winstub* below.

Auberge du Gueberschwihr Ⓗ Ⓡ
12 rue Basse, 68420 Gueberschwihr. Tel 03 89 49 35 45. Ⓕ
Good, honest food and simple bedrooms in a charming house.

Klein Ⓗ Ⓡ
44 rue de la Vallée, 68570 Soultzmatt. Tel 03 89 47 00 10; fax 03 89 47 65 03. Ⓕ Ⓕ Ⓕ
Simple, comfortable hotel with large bedrooms. In the top-quality restaurant, an impressive wine list, with wines from both Alsace and Bordeaux, accompanies classic local dishes.

Le Caveau Morakopf Ⓡ
7 rue des Trois Épis, 68230 Niedermorschwihr. Tel 03 89 27 09 78; fax 03 89 27 08 63. Ⓕ
Excellent, popular *winstub* serving good regional dishes and local wines. Book ahead.

Auberge du Père Floranc Ⓗ Ⓡ
9 rue Herzog, 68000 Wettolsheim. Tel 03 89 80 79 14; fax 03 89 79 77 00. Ⓕ Ⓕ
Family-run inn serving good classic food. Very good wine list at reasonable prices.

La Petite Palette Ⓡ
16 rue de Bâle, 68600 Neuf-Brisach. Tel 03 89 72 73 50; fax 03 89 73 61 93. Ⓕ Ⓕ
Henri Gagneux is a talented young chef offering superb food and well-chosen wines, all at reasonable prices.

Hôtel au Soleil Ⓗ
20 rue Ste-Gertrude, 68000 Wettolsheim. Tel 03 89 80 62 66. Ⓕ
Simple and peaceful hotel.

Auberge du Veilleur Ⓡ
12 place Turenne, 68230 Turckheim. Tel 03 89 27 32 22; fax 03 89 27 55 56. Ⓕ
Warm welcome, family cooking and local wines.

Wines and Wine Villages

The wine route continues south of Colmar through many picturesque villages, some of which are tucked away in quiet side valleys leading up to the heavily forested Vosges, which are steeper in this southern section.

Bergholtz (Grand Cru: Spiegel) A small wine village, whose vineyards run on from those of Guebwiller.
Best producer: DIRLER.

Eguisheim (Grands Crus: Eichberg and Pfersigberg) This fortified village with double octagonal ramparts has one of the largest areas of Grand Cru vineyards in Alsace. It is renowned for both Gewurztraminer and Riesling.
Best producers: Charles Baur, BEYER, EGUISHEIM *co-operative,* GINGLINGER, *Sorg*.

Gueberschwihr (Grand Cru: Goldert) Up in the hills, this fortified village has been famous for wine since the 8th century and produces superb Muscat and Gewurztraminer.
Best producers: BURN, *Bernard Humbrecht*.

Guebwiller (Grands Crus: Kessler, Kitterlé, Saering and Spiegel) On the river Lauch, much of Guebwiller has been spoilt by textile and chemical industries, but it still has some fine buildings and a walk up the pretty Lauch Valley, also known as Florival, is recommended. Guebwiller has more Grands Crus than any village in Alsace. Domaines Schlumberger dominates wine-making here.
Best producer: SCHLUMBERGER.

Husseren-les-Châteaux
Overlooking Eguisheim and with wonderful panoramic views, Husseren is the highest point of the Alsace vineyards. The 3 ruined châteaux on the skyline above the vineyards are called the Tours d'Eguisheim.
Best producers: KUENTZ-BAS, *Lieber, Scherer, Schueller*.

Kaysersberg (Grand Cru: Schlossberg) A beautiful village whose name means Caesar's Peak, illustrating its Roman origins. Its vineyards are famous for Gewurztraminer.
Best producer: WEINBACH.

Kientzheim (Grands Crus: Furstentum and Schlossberg) Alsace's main wine museum is in the castle which is owned by the local wine fraternity.
Best producers: ANDRÉ BLANCK, PAUL BLANCK.

Niedermorschwihr (Grand Cru: Sommerberg) Small village best known for its Riesling, especially from the steep, relatively sheltered slopes of the Sommerberg Grand Cru.
Best producer: BOXLER.

Orschwihr (Grand Cru: Pfingstberg) Built on terraces, with some fine Renaissance houses. Gewurztraminer and Pinot Gris do especially well here.
Best producers: ALBRECHT, *François Braun*.

Pfaffenheim (Grand Cru: Steinert) The lesser Alsace grape varieties, such as Pinot Blanc and Sylvaner, are particularly successful here.
Best producers: Frick, PFAFFENHEIM *co-operative, Rieflé*.

Rouffach (Grand Cru: Vorbourg) Red sandstone is dominant in this village, which has fine Renaissance buildings.
Best producer: MURÉ.

Soultzmatt (Grand Cru: Zinnkoepflé) Lying in a very pretty valley, Soultzmatt has a particularly warm climate which favours Gewurztraminer.
Best producers: Boesch, LANDMANN.

Thann (Grand Cru: Rangen) Thann's very steep vineyards were well known as early as the 12th century. The orientation of the terraced slope and volcanic soil combine almost to roast Rangen's grapes in some years. The Riesling and Pinot Gris are magnificent.
Best producers: SCHOFFIT, ZIND-HUMBRECHT.

Turckheim (Grand Cru: Brand) This fortified wine village still maintains the tradition of the night watchman in summer.
Best producers: CHARLES SCHLERET, TURCKHEIM *co-operative*, ZIND-HUMBRECHT.

Wettolsheim (Grand Cru: Steingrubler) Possibly the site of the first Alsace vineyard, planted by the Romans.
Best producers: BARMÈS-BUECHER, *Albert Mann*.

Wintzenheim (Grand Cru: Hengst) Surrounded by excellent vineyards, but on a main road, so not such an attractive village.
Best producer: JOSMEYER.

The Zinnkoepflé Grand Cru occupies a long, sheltered slope above the village of Soultzmatt.

A–Z of Main Wine Producers

Two-thirds of the 250 million bottles of Champagne that are produced, on average, every year are sold by the houses, or *négociants*, who own only about 12 per cent of the region's vineyards. The rest of the vineyards are divided among thousands of small growers, who may make their own wine, sell grapes to the houses, or take their grapes to a co-operative to have their wine made.

Most producers in Alsace belong to one of three main categories. The best-known names are mostly those of the merchants, or *négociants*, who usually own vineyards but also produce wine from grapes or wine purchased from smaller growers. The co-operatives are powerful in Alsace and they make and sell wines for a large number of grape growers. Finally, there are many, usually small-scale producers (only a few possess more than 20ha), who make wine solely from their own vineyards. The following is a selection of the leading producers in both regions.

Key to Symbols

Visiting arrangements ⊘ Visitors welcome ⊘ By appointment ⊗ No visitors.
Wine styles made ⦿ Red wine ⦿ White wine ⦿ Rosé wine ⦿ Sparkling wine.
Page numbers refer to the tour featuring the producer.

Domaine Lucien Albrecht
9 Grand Rue, 68500 Orschwihr. Tel 03 89 76 95 18; fax 03 89 76 20 22. ⊘⦿⦿⦿ pp.66, 69
This dynamic family estate has a considerable vineyard holding in the southern part of Alsace. Jean Albrecht, who runs the estate, is the young mayor of Orschwihr. The wide range of wines includes particularly fine Rieslings and Pinot Gris, as well as superb Vendanges Tardives. The well-kept winery has a pleasant tasting room and offers a friendly welcome.

Arnold
16 rue de la Paix, 67650 Dambach-la-Ville. Tel 03 88 92 41 70; fax 03 88 92 62 95. ⊘⦿ pp.54, 59
The young Arnold couple trained in Burgundy and make an excellent range of Alsace wines, with forward fruit flavours. Their vineyards include some of the Frankstein Grand Cru.

Michel Arnould et Fils
28 rue de Mailly, 51360 Verzenay. Tel 03 26 49 40 06; fax 03 26 49 44 61. ⊘⦿ pp.17, 21
Verzenay is one of the villages on the Montagne de Reims that faces north. In theory, this may not seem ideal for ripening grapes, but nevertheless it produces some of the finest in Champagne, full of style and some powerful acidity. The wines of the Arnould father-and-son team show the strong acidity typical of this north-facing village, which gives them considerable aging capacity.

François Principe Arnoult
51480 Fleury-la-Rivière. Tel 03 26 58 42 53; fax 03 26 52 75 81. ⊘⦿ pp.29, 31
This Champagne co-operative is worth a visit for the splendid murals and well-organized tours. The wines are well made.

L Aubry Fils
4–6 Grande Rue, 51390 Jouy-lès-Reims. Tel 03 26 49 20 07; fax 03 26 49 75 27. ⊘⦿ pp.15, 21
Easy to find by the luminous sign in an otherwise fairly empty village, this go-ahead family grower makes an excellent range of Champagnes. Some of these, such as the un-dosed rosé, are remarkable and unusual. The tasting includes an interesting visit to the old cellars.

Paul Bara
4 rue Yvonnet, 51150 Bouzy. Tel 03 26 57 00 50; fax 03 26 57 81 24. ⊘⦿⦿⦿ pp.18, 21
Bouzy is one of the top villages in the Montagne de Reims and the Bara family make single-village wines with very full fruit flavours. This is precisely the opposite approach to that of the big Champagne houses, which blend wines from many villages.

Barmès-Buecher
30 rue Ste-Gertrude, 68920 Wettolsheim. Tel 03 89 80 62 92; fax 03 89 79 30 80. ⊘⦿⦿ pp.64, 69
This friendly and enthusiastic young couple make rich, aromatic Alsace wines that drink well when they are young and tend to have a full, slightly sweet edge to them.

E Barnault
2 rue Gambetta, 51150 Bouzy. Tel 03 26 57 09 97; fax 03 26 57 01 54. ⊘⦿⦿ pp.18, 21
These are full-flavoured Champagnes from the excellent Grand Cru vineyards of Bouzy. The Barnault family also produce a decent Bouzy Rouge, the local still wine of the Coteaux Champenois appellation.

Baron-Albert
Grand Porteron, 12310 Charly-sur-Marne. Tel 03 23 82 02 65; fax 03 23 82 02 44. ⊘⦿ pp.28, 31
This is almost the first Champagne producer you reach in the Marne Valley when driving from Paris. The

excellent, crisp Champagnes come from extensive hillside vineyards and there is an impressive cellar, hand-dug by the owner's father.

Baron-Fuenté

21 avenue Fernand-Drouet, 02310 Charly-sur-Marne. Tel 03 23 82 01 97; fax 03 23 82 12 00. ⊘① pp.28, 31
Another branch of the Baron family specializes in fairly full, fruity Champagnes, based on Pinot Meunier. There are also some serious vintage wines that will age well.

André Beaufort

1 rue de Vaudemanges, 51150 Ambonnay. Tel 03 26 57 01 50; fax 03 26 52 83 50. ⊘①⊕p.21
Jacques Beaufort owns vines at Ambonnay on the Montagne de Reims and also further south in the Aube region. They are cultivated without pesticides and his Champagnes are complex and will appeal to connoisseurs. They are sold under the name André Beaufort, as well as his own.

Léon Beyer

2 rue de la 1ère Armée, 68420 Eguisheim. Tel 03 89 41 41 05; fax 03 89 23 93 63. ⊘⊕① pp.64, 69
The Beyer family has owned vineyards at Eguisheim since 1580. The current firm now makes a range of outstanding, powerful wines, including

Gewurztraminer of great staying power and steely Rieslings. You can taste in the shop in the village, but make an appointment if you want to visit the winery.

Billecart-Salmon

40 rue Carnot, 51160 Mareuil-sur-Ay. Tel 03 26 52 60 22; fax 03 26 52 64 88. ⊘① pp.18, 21
This is one of the best Champagne houses, and yet it is relatively unknown, possibly because it is slightly off the beaten track. Grapes come from a small vineyard holding, as well as being purchased from the Montagne de Reims and upper Marne Valley. The very well-made wines are extremely elegant, fresh and delicate. The vintage Cuvée N-F Billecart is especially good.

André Blanck et Fils

5 rue Golbery, 68240 Kientzheim. Tel 03 89 78 24 72; fax 03 89 47 17 07. ⊘① p.69
This grower makes particularly good Schlossberg Grand Cru and fine Pinot Gris, called Clos Schwendi after the Alsatian soldier, de Schwendi, who supposedly brought back the first Pinot Gris vines to Alsace.

Paul Blanck et Fils

32 Grand Rue, 68240 Kientzheim. Tel 03 89 78 23 56; fax 03 89 47 16 45. ⊘⊕① pp.62, 69
An excellent Alsace estate, also known as Domaine des Comtes de Lupfen, which specializes in a minerally, austere style of wine, made to age for a few years. Riesling Schlossberg and Pinot Gris Furstentum are often the best but the range is very wide.

Bollinger

16 rue Jules Lobet, 51160 Ay. Tel 03 26 53 33 66; fax 03 26 54 85 59. ⊘①⊕ pp.19, 21
This is one of the undisputed stars of Champagne, with wines that pay respect to tradition, some of them being fermented or aged in barrels, while accepting the contribution of modern techniques. Bollinger's family structure and voluntarily limited production are becoming only too rare among the Champagne houses. There is a wonderful range of wines, whose strong personalities may not be to all tastes, or, in the case of the Vieilles Vignes, for all pockets. There is glorious vintage RD, which means that the wine has been left to age on its lees for longer than usual before disgorgement, picking up loads of flavour on the way.

Albert Boxler

78 rue des Trois Épis, 68230 Niedermorschwihr. Tel 03 89 27 11 32; fax 03 89 27 11 32. ⊘① p.69
The granite-based soils of Albert Boxler's vineyards in the Brand and Sommerberg Grands Crus result in very fine and aromatic wines, particularly Riesling.

Maison Ernest Burn

14 rue Basse, 68420 Gueberschwihr. Tel 03 89 49 20 68; fax 03 89 49 28 56. ⊘① pp.66, 69
In one of the most beautiful houses in this attractive Alsace village, the Burn brothers make superb and expressive wines, particularly from Clos St-Imer, a vineyard within the Goldert Grand Cru. There is a fine vaulted cellar-cum-tasting room.

VISITING WINE PRODUCERS

Telephone in advance to small producers to ensure that your visit is convenient and that there will be someone there to receive you.
English-speaking guides conduct visits in the larger Champagne houses and co-operatives. At the smaller estates the owner or winemaker is more likely to show you around; he/she will be more knowledgeable about the domaine, but possibly less fluent in English.

Lunchtime in rural France is still an important occasion, so ensure that you don't arrive at a property between 12 and 2pm.
Holidays are often taken in August and consequently the wineries may be closed for visits.
Harvest time (early September/mid-October) is a busy time of the year and people may not always have time to stop to help you. Visits are not recommended unless the producer employs a full-time guide.
Tastings will probably consist of

samples of the most recently bottled vintage(s). These will be available for purchase at the smaller domaines but not necessarily at the great estates. Do not expect a range of older vintages.
Spittoons are usually provided at tastings, and whether or not you are driving, it is best to make use of them in order to keep a clean palate.
Credit cards are not always accepted as payment for wine purchases, particularly at the smaller properties.

de Castellane
57 rue de Verdun, 51204
Épernay. Tel 03 26 55 15 33;
fax 03 26 54 24 81. ✓ ① p.24
This family-run Champagne
house is famous for the amazing
architecture of its tower which
can be seen from all over
Épernay. It houses a collection of
old Champagne posters and
labels. The Champagne is good,
too, with excellent vintage
(especially the prestige cuvée
Florens de Castellane) and non-
vintage cuvées.

Cattier
6 rue Dom Pérignon, 51500
Chigny-les-Roses. Tel 03 26 03
42 11; fax 03 26 03 43 13. ✓ ①
pp.17, 21
This small family-run
Champagne house, making
robust wines, owns the Clos du
Moulin, one of Champagne's
few *clos*, or vineyards enclosed by
walls. The impressive cellars
have been carved out of the
chalk in a variety of different
architectural styles.

Guy Charlemagne
4 rue de la Brèche d'Oger, 51190
le Mesnil-sur-Oger. Tel 03 26 57
52 98; fax 03 26 57 97 81. ✓ ①
pp.38, 39
One of the star growers of this
village, where competition is
fierce, Guy Charlemagne and his
son Philippe make excellent
vintage Champagnes and lighter
non-vintage wines.

Charlier et Fils
4 rue des Pervenches, 51700
Montigny-sous-Châtillon. Tel 03
26 58 35 15; fax 03 26 58 02 31.
✓ ① pp.29, 31
There are some excellent, full-
flavoured Champagnes, rounded
out by dosage, from this pleasant
grower's establishment that has a
lot to offer the visitor, such as an
unusual garden in the form of a
map of the Champagne area.

Jacky Charpentier
88 rue de Rueil, 51700 Villers-
sur-Châtillon. Tel 03 26 58 05
78; fax 03 26 58 36 59. ✓ ①
pp.29, 31
Do not be disconcerted by the
location (a modern house on a

housing-estate extension to this
village devoted to Champagne-
making). Jacky Charpentier and
his wife are very welcoming and
their Champagnes are fruity and
well made, as well as being
excellent value.

Marc Chauvet
1–3 rue de la Liberté, 51500
Rilly-la-Montagne. Tel 03 26 03
42 71; fax 03 26 03 42 38. ✓ ①
pp.17, 21
This grower with 12ha of vines
in the northern part of the
Montagne de Reims makes
Champagnes of considerable
freshness as the wines do not
undergo malolactic fermentation.

Gaston Chiquet
912 avenue du Général Leclerc,
51530 Dizy. Tel 03 26 55 22 02;
fax 03 26 51 83 81. ✓ ① p.21
Gaston Chiquet is another
branch of the family that owns
Jacquesson. He uses an unusually
high proportion of Chardonnay
and Pinot Meunier for the
Montagne de Reims area and
the wines are rather full-bodied
with a rounded flavour due to
the origin of the grapes and a
sometimes generous dosage.

Dehu Père et Fils
3 rue St-Georges, 02650 Fossoy.
Tel 03 23 71 90 47; fax 03 23 71
88 91. ✓ ① pp.28, 31
An enterprising family business
which is well organized for
visitors and has an interesting
museum. Its Champagne is well
made by the local co-operative,
which also produces the Pannier
brand.

Domaine Marcel Deiss
15 route du Vin, 68750 Bergheim.
Tel 03 89 73 63 37; fax 03 89 73
32 67. ✓ ① pp.54, 59
Jean-Michel Deiss is one of the
most fervent protagonists in
Alsace of low yields and
authentic wines that show their
origin. A wide range of styles
includes well-made generic
Alsace through to sumptuous
Sélection de Grains Nobles.

Delamotte Père et Fils
7 rue de la Brèche d'Oger, 51190
le Mesnil-sur-Oger. Tel 03 26 57

51 65; fax 03 26 57 79 29. ✓ ①
pp.37, 39
This is a very old Champagne
house which has remained quite
small, although it now belongs
to Laurent-Perrier. Situated next
door to its sister house, Salon, it
makes some extremely good-
value and elegant Champagnes,
many of which are made from
Chardonnay alone.

Deutz
16 rue Jeanson, 51160 Ay. Tel 03
26 55 15 11; fax 03 26 54 01 21.
✓ ① pp.19, 21
This family-run Champagne
house, with fine vineyards mainly
in the Montagne de Reims, has
recently been bought by
Roederer, which can only help
to reinforce its high quality.
Most of the wines contain a large
proportion of Pinot Noir. The
non-vintage is always reliable but
the top wine is the weightier
Blanc de Blancs, the Cuvée
William Deutz.

Jean-Pierre Dirler
13 rue d'Issenheim, 68500
Bergholtz. Tel 03 89 76 91 00;
fax 03 89 76 85 97. ✓ ① pp.67,
69
This small but high-quality
producer owns land in the steep-
sided Kessler, Saering and
Spiegel Grands Crus which
cover a variety of soils. His wines
are superb, especially the
Riesling, with full, soft flavours
and a good backbone that allows
them to age well.

Dopff et Irion
Ch. de Riquewihr, 68340
Riquewihr. Tel 03 89 47 92 51;
fax 03 89 47 98 90. ✓ ① ① ①
pp.56, 59
Based in the Ch. de Riquewihr,
this is one of Alsace's largest
firms. In 1997 it was taken over
by the Cave de Pfaffenheim.
The best wines come from its
own vineyards at Riquewihr.

Dopff au Moulin
2 avenue Jacques Preiss, 68340
Riquewihr. Tel 03 89 47 92 23;
fax 03 89 47 83 61. ✔️🔵📷📷
pp.56, 59
One of the biggest *négociants* in
Alsace, Dopff au Moulin also has
extensive vineyards of its own. It
is so well-known for its
pioneering role in the creation of
Crémant d'Alsace that its table
wines are often, unjustly,
overlooked. The best come
under the Domaines Dopff label.

Étienne Doué
11 rue de Troyes, 10300
Montgueux. Tel 03 25 74 84 41;
fax 03 25 79 00 47. ✔️📷 p.45
This small grower makes
reasonably priced, straightforward
Champagnes in a little-known
area near Troyes that supplies
excellent Chardonnay grapes to
several famous houses.

Drappier
10200 Urville. Tel 03 25 27 40
15; fax 03 25 27 41 19. ✔️📷
pp.43, 45
A long-established, family-run
Champagne house, with
activities in the Montagne de
Reims that complement its main
base in the Aube. As well as
magnificent medieval cellars in
Urville, there is an interesting
range of Champagnes, including
some older vintages.

R Dumont et Fils
Bas des Perrières, 10200
Champignol-lez-Mondéville.
Tel 03 25 27 45 95; fax 03 25 27
45 97. ✔️📷 pp.43, 45
With its 22ha and modern
equipment, this exemplary
medium-sized grower's business
shows how good the Aube
Champagnes can be. These ones
are fresh, supple and easy to drink.

Égly-Ouriet
9–15 rue de Trépail, 51150
Ambonnay. Tel 03 26 57 00 70;
fax 03 26 57 06 52. ✔️📷🔵p.21

Michel Égly has a small but well-
sited Grand Cru vineyard at
Ambonnay. Excellent, traditional
viticulture is still carried out –
the land is ploughed between the
vines, which are unusually old
for Champagne. The wines have
an accordingly high
concentration of flavours and
will age well after disgorgement.
There is also an interesting
collection of old vineyard tools.

Cave Vinicole d'Eguisheim
68420 Eguisheim. Tel 03 89 22
20 20; fax 03 89 23 47 09.
✔️🔵📷📷 pp.64, 69
Based in a large building at the
entrance to one of the loveliest
villages in Alsace, this co-
operative is the giant producer in
Alsace, as it makes about 10 per
cent of the region's wines.
Production is varied and many of
the wines are sold under the
Wolfberger brand name. Grands
Crus Gewurztraminer and
Riesling Seigneurs d'Eguisheim
are excellent wines. Visits here
are well-organized.

Gaidoz-Forget
1 rue Carnot, 51500 Ludes.
Tel 03 26 61 13 03; fax 03 26 61
11 65. ✔️📷📷🔵 p.21
This grower makes full-bodied,
firm Champagnes, mainly from
Pinot Noir and Meunier. There
is an interesting Champagne rosé.

Gatinois
7 rue Marcel Mailly, 51160 Ay.
Tel 03 26 55 14 26; fax 03 26 52
75 99. ✔️📷📷 pp.19, 21
This small, family-run
Champagne house has vines in
the heart of Ay. The top-quality
wines are full and rich in flavour,
true to grapes from Ay, one of
the most famous of all
Champagne villages. The owner,
Pierre Cheval-Gatinois, sells
some of his grapes to Bollinger,
which gives one an idea of the
high quality of the raw material.
There is also an excellent red
Coteaux Champenois.

René Geoffroy
150 rue Bois-des-Jots, 51480
Cumières. Tel 03 26 55 32 31;
fax 03 16 54 66 50. ✔️📷📷🔵 p.31
This family-run Champagne

business practises traditional
wine-making in large oak barrels
or *foudres*, without malolactic
fermentation. The grape
proportions vary considerably
according to the blend. There is
excellent vintage and good non-
vintage Champagne and some
Cumières red.

Armand Gilg et Fils
2–4 rue Rotland, 67140
Mittelbergheim. Tel 03 88 08 92
76; fax 03 88 08 25 91. ✔️📷📷
pp.53, 59
In this tiny Alsace wine village,
Armand Gilg makes good wines,
including particularly fine
Crémant d'Alsace.

Pierre Gimonnet et Fils
1 rue de la République, 51530
Cuis. Tel 03 26 59 78 70; fax 02
36 59 79 84. ✔️📷 pp.34, 39
Made from some of the best
vineyards in the Côte des Blancs,
at Cramant, Cuis and Chouilly,
the Gimonnet family's
Champagnes are technically
perfect and extremely pure in
their flavours. The vintage wines
age well.

Paul Ginglinger
8 place Charles de Gaulle, 68420
Eguisheim. Tel 03 89 41 44 25;
fax 03 89 24 94 88. ✔️🔵📷📷
pp.64, 69
It is worth walking to the top of
the village to Paul Ginglinger's
light, airy tasting room to see
how successfully traditional and
modern styles of architecture can
blend in Alsace. The fine décor
is more than matched by superb
wines of great freshness. The
wines are mostly of the very dry
style and are beautifully crafted,
especially the powerful and
surprisingly rich Grand Cru
Riesling Pfersigberg.

Gonet-Sulcova
13 rue Henri Martin, 51200
Épernay. Tel 03 26 54 37 63;
fax 03 26 55 36 71. ✔️📷 p.34
Many members of the Gonet
family are involved in making
Champagne. This branch lives in
Épernay, which is unusual for a
small grower. Their vineyards
nearby produce delicate wines,
with an excellent Blanc de Blancs.

Gosset

69 rue Jules Blondeau, 51160 Ay.
Tel 03 26 56 99 56; fax 03 26 51
55 88. ✓① pp.19, 21
Arguably the oldest Champagne
house of all, Gosset is a medium-
sized firm now owned by the
Cointreau family. There is a
wide range of cask-fermented
Champagnes of great character,
made with a high proportion of
Pinot Noir and long cellaring.
The house style is rich and
heavy, old-fashioned perhaps but
lushly enjoyable all the same.

Alfred Gratien

30 rue Maurice Cervaux, 51201
Épernay. Tel 03 26 54 38 20;
fax 03 26 54 53 44. ✓① p.24
This little-known house makes
some of the most superb
traditional Champagnes. Fairly
austere in their youth, owing to
barrel fermentation (rare
nowadays) and a lack of
malolactic fermentation which
softens wines, they are gloriously
fragrant and powerful after a few
years. The top wines are all one
could ask for, and the standard
non-vintage is usually 4 years old
when sold, rather than the more
normal 3. A visit here is a
memorable experience if you
like this style of Champagne but
the buildings are low-key and
the atmosphere workmanlike. At
Alfred Gratien the money goes
into the wine rather than into
showing off.

Jean-Noël Haton

5 rue Jean Mermoz, 51480
Damery. Tel 03 26 58 40 45.
✓① p.31
This small Champagne *négociant*
also owns about 12ha of vines.
The good Cuvée Prestige is
made from equal amounts of
Pinot Noir and Chardonnay.

Charles Heidsieck

4 boulevard Henry Vasnier, 51100
Reims. Tel 03 26 84 43 50;
fax 03 26 84 43 86 ✓① p.13
Under new owners, Rémy
Martin, a lot of effort has gone
into improving the quality of the
Champagne in recent years. The
non-vintage Brut is one of the
most consistently reliable among
the Grandes Marques. It is fairly

full-bodied, largely due to a high
proportion of reserve wines and
excellent wine-making.
Although the vineyard holding is
small, the art of blending is
perfectly practised here. There is
superb vintage Blanc de Blancs.

Henriot

3 place des Droits de l'Homme,
51100 Reims. Tel 03 26 89 53
00; fax 03 26 89 53 10. ✓①
p.13
This is one of Champagne's very
rare family-owned Grandes
Marques. The basis for the blend
is a magnificent vineyard spread
mainly throughout the Côte des
Blancs that produces elegant
wines. The fine cellars in Reims
are carved out of the chalk
subsoil.

Pierre Hering

6 rue Sultzer, 67140 Barr. Tel 03
88 08 90 07; fax 03 88 08 08 54
✓① pp.53, 59
This is a typical, small Alsace
family winery, with barrels and
tanks up and down the stairs and
a small tasting room. Pierre
Hering has been making great
strides recently and there are
some fine wines in a dry, almost
austere style. The Sylvaner Clos
de la Folie Marco and the
Riesling Grand Cru Kirchberg
are the best wines.

Hugel et Fils

3 rue de la Première Armée,
68340 Riquewihr. Tel 03 89 47
92 15; fax 03 89 49 00 10.
✓①① pp.56, 59
This traditional house with a
long-standing reputation is
perhaps the most famous wine
name in Alsace, thanks to
assiduous marketing and (most of
the time) the quality of the
wines. If you call ahead, you
may be shown around by a
member of the Hugel family, but
you can also taste in the
company's shop. There is a
wonderful collection of old
wines and rich Vendanges
Tardives and Sélections de
Grains Nobles are a speciality.

Jacquesson et Fils

68 rue du Colonel Fabien,
51530 Dizy. Tel 03 26 55 68 11;

fax 03 26 51 06 25. ✓① pp.19,
21
With its walled grounds and an
interesting mixture of old and
modern décor, this is a delightful
Champagne house to visit and
deserves to be better known.
Owned by a branch of the
Chiquet family, it produces some
very well made wines of strong
personality, and, unusually,
releases some vintages when they
are perfectly mature.

Josmeyer

76 rue Clémenceau, 68920
Wintzenheim. Tel 03 89 27 91
90; fax 03 89 27 91 99. ●①
pp.64, 69
Based in a beautiful building set
around a courtyard, the *négociant*
Josmeyer has a pronounced
aesthetic sense that shows in the
décor, the labels and even the
wines, which are made to
harmonize with food. The range
is bafflingly wide, with some
names that may be hard to
understand, but there is always a
reason behind them, such as the
date of bottling. Both from its
own grapes and others,
Josmeyer's wines are excellent,
even from less prestigious
varieties such as Auxerrois.

Juillet-Lallement

30 rue Carnot, 51380 Verzy.
Tel 03 26 97 91 09; fax 03 26 97
93 29. ✓① pp.17, 21
This small grower has a tiny
vineyard in one of Champagne's
star villages for Pinot Noir,
where many of the big houses
have extensive vineyard
holdings. These are very lightly
dosed Champagnes that need
some time to come around.

André Kientzler

50 route de Bergheim,
Ribeauvillé. Tel 03 89 73 67 10;
fax 03 89 73 35 81. ✓① p.59

Very fine vineyards in 3 Grands Crus provide the top range of Kientzler's wines, but the basic ones are also good. A scrupulous winemaker, he makes one of the best Rieslings in Alsace, from the Grand Cru Geisberg.

Marc Kreydenweiss
12 rue Deharbe, 67140 Andlau. Tel 03 88 08 95 83; fax 03 88 08 41 16. ⊘●①① pp.53, 59
Easy to find, with a small shop opposite the church, Marc Kreydenweiss is one of the most thoughtful of Alsace's winemakers. He has always experimented and his vineyard is now run on biodynamic lines. The wines are pure expressions of their terroir, in a style which is vibrant and full-flavoured but perfectly dry. These are definitely wines for keeping.

Krug
5 rue Coquebert, 51150 Reims. Tel 03 26 84 44 20; fax 03 26 84 44 49. ⊘① pp.15, 37
Krug is a serious, and seriously expensive, Champagne house. Apart from Gratien, it is the only house to ferment all its wines in small barrels. Indeed, a barrel-maker is employed to keep them in good repair, since new oak is not used. The art of blending is brought to perfection here. The Champagnes are aged for far longer than most before being released and have a special vibrancy, power and complexity that makes them unique. The non-vintage, called Grande Cuvée, is far better than most and there is also an excellent vintage and a single-vineyard Clos du Mesnil Blanc de Blancs.

Kuentz-Bas
14 route du Vin, 68420 Husseren-les-Châteaux. Tel 03 89 49 30 24; fax 03 89 49 23 39. ⊘●①① pp.65, 69
Run by the Bas and Weber families this small Alsace *négociant*

also owns 18ha of vineyards (these wines are labelled Réserve Personelle). The wines are richly perfumed and generally luscious and there are excellent Pinot Gris and Gewurztraminer Vendange Tardive wines.

Jean Lallement
1 rue Moët, 51360 Verzenay. Tel 03 26 49 43 52; fax 03 26 54 11 98. ⊘① pp.17, 21
This Champagne grower owns a tiny vineyard of less than 5ha which is devoted almost entirely to Pinot Noir in one of the best villages for this grape. Jean Lallement's Champagnes need a bit of bottle age for the clear, delicate aromas to develop as the terroir of Verzenay is known for its austerity.

Seppi Landmann
20 rue de la Vallée, 68570 Soultzmatt. Tel 03 89 47 09 33; fax 03 89 47 06 99. ⊘①① pp.66, 69
Seppi Landmann is one of Alsace's great wine-making characters: a Rabelaisian figure who makes excellent wines entirely from his own grapes grown in this delightful valley. The wines tend to be made in a dry, lively style, but there are many variations within the range. He sells single-vineyard top wines at keen prices as futures.

Guy Larmandier
30 rue Général Koenig, 51130 Vertus. Tel 03 26 52 12 41; fax 03 26 52 19 38. ⊘① pp.38, 39
This Champagne firm in the Côte des Blancs is run by a brother-and-sister team, François and Colette Larmandier. The vines are divided between Cramant and Vertus and the wines are particularly delicate and fine. Tasting takes place in a homely kitchen.

Laurent-Perrier
Avenue de Champagne, 51150 Tours-sur-Marne. Tel 03 26 58 91 22; fax 03 26 58 77 29. ⊘①①●① pp.18, 21, 37
Unlike other big Champagne houses, this family-owned firm is sited in the vineyards on the

edge of this small town. It can probably boast the fastest rate of growth of any house over the past 30 years or so and the style is modern and easy to appreciate. The non-vintage Brut is delightfully fresh and full of fruit, and there is also a rare un-dosed Champagne, the very fine Ultra-Brut and a deliciously fruity rosé. The visit is informative.

Lilbert Fils
223 rue du Moutier, 51530 Cramant. Tel 03 26 57 50 16; fax 03 26 58 93 86. ⊘① pp.35–6, 39
Hidden away in a side street in Cramant, Georges Lilbert produces some pure, delicious Champagnes from his vineyards around the village. Informal and friendly welcome in a tiny office.

Gustave Lorentz
35 Grand' Rue, 68750 Bergheim. Tel 03 89 73 22 22; fax 03 89 73 30 49. ⊘① pp.55, 59
One of the pillars of the traditional *négociant* scene in Alsace and also owning 27ha of vines, Lorentz tends to make full-bodied, rich-flavoured wines with a fair amount of residual sugar. He is particularly renowned for Gewurztraminer.

Mailly Grand Cru
28 rue de la Libération, 51500 Mailly-Champagne. Tel 03 26 49 41 10; fax 03 26 49 42 27. ⊘① pp.17, 21
This Champagne co-operative owns 70ha of prime vineyards, mostly Pinot Noir, at Mailly and the grapes are much sought-after by the Grande Marque houses. The wines age well and are reliable and good value.

Margaine
3 avenue de Champagne, 51380 Villers-Marmery. Tel 03 26 97 92 13; fax 03 26 97 97 45. ⊘① pp.18, 21

Villers-Marmery is unusual within the Montagne de Reims, since the village has extensive plantings of Chardonnay. This shows in the Champagnes of growers such as Margaine, who uses 90 per cent of this white grape in his blend.

Serge Mathieu
10340 Avirey-Lingey. Tel 03 25 29 32 58; fax 03 25 29 11 57. ✓①① pp.44, 45
This Aube grower makes extremely reliable, excellent Champagne. The non-vintage Blanc de Noirs is superb, and all the wines are harmoniously balanced. The premises are neat and welcoming and bed and breakfast is available.

José Michel et Fils
14 rue Prélot, 51530 Moussy. Tel 03 26 54 04 69; fax 03 26 55 37 12. ✓① p.34
José Michel is a dynamic Champagne grower based just south of Épernay with 20ha of vines, mainly Pinot Meunier. The style is generally light and fruity, easy to drink, with some extra depth to the vintage wines.

Frédéric Mochel
56 rue Principale, 67310 Traenheim. Tel 03 88 50 38 67; fax 03 88 50 56 19. ✓① pp.50, 59
Frédéric Mochel specializes in dry, elegant Riesling that ages well and also makes very good Muscat. A visit here is an excellent introduction to Alsace – the welcome is warm, the half-timbered buildings typical of the region, and you feel you are entering a home and an impeccably run place of work at the same time.

Moët et Chandon
20 avenue de Champagne, 51220 Épernay. Tel 03 26 51 20 20; fax 03 26 51 20 37. ✓①①① pp.24, 29
Now part of the enormous LVMH group, this is the giant of Champagne, with on average more than 24 million bottles produced every year and over 28km (17 miles) of cellars to house its stocks. The wines are

fairly supple, with a distinctively greenish aroma that makes them easy to recognize. The vintage wine is more consistent, as is the Dom Pérignon, the name of Moët's famous de luxe Champagne. The huge building in the avenue de Champagne is very well equipped for visits. Moët also owns the abbey at Hautvillers.

Pierre Moncuit
11 rue Persault-Maheu, 51190 le Mesnil-sur-Oger. Tel 03 26 57 52 65; fax 03 26 57 97 89. ✓① pp.38, 39
As befits a specialist grower in the heart of the Côte des Blancs, the dominant colour of the Champagne here is white. A brother-and-sister team, Yves and Nicole Moncuit, runs this family business, which has impressive cellars and makes some excellent Blanc de Blancs Champagnes, with fine aromas.

Morel Père et Fils
93 rue Général de Gaulle, 10340 les Riceys. Tel 03 25 29 10 88; fax 03 25 29 66 72. ✓①① pp.44, 45
This excellent grower in the southern Aube makes rare Rosé des Riceys with wonderful, heady Pinot Noir aromas and flavours and which ages well. There is also good Champagne.

René Muré
Clos St-Landelin, route du Vin, 68250 Rouffach. Tel 03 89 78 58 00; fax 03 89 78 58 01. ✓①①① pp.66, 69
Muré's tasting room looks out over the superb terraced vineyard of Clos St-Landelin, within the Grand Cru Vorbourg. This forms the major part of the vineyard holding of this *négociant* house. Using very ripe grapes, the wines are superb, more complex than fruity, and there is excellent Muscat, Riesling, Gewurztraminer and Pinot Noir.

Domaine Ostertag
87 rue Finckwiller, 67680 Epfig. Tel 03 88 85 51 34; fax 03 88 85 58 95. ✓① pp.53, 59
André Ostertag is an enthusiastic and unconventional winemaker whose approach to wine-making is creative not traditional. If you are looking for Alsace wines of personality, make an appointment to taste here. From severely restricted yields, the wines are pure, full of character and yet easy to drink. Painting, writing and sculpture form part of the surroundings as you taste in a beautiful light room.

Bruno Paillard
Avenue de Champagne, 51100 Reims. Tel 03 26 36 20 22; fax 03 26 36 57 72. ✓①
This recently founded but highly acclaimed Champagne house exports over 90 per cent of its production. A small, specialized and consistent range of wines is made in modern cellars, from grapes bought from over 30 villages. Wine-making is meticulous and all the wines are made in a Brut style with minimum dosage.

Palmer
67 rue Jacquart, 51100 Reims. Tel 03 26 07 35 07; fax 03 26 07 45 24. ✓①
An interesting Champagne co-operative which has made a considerable effort to produce consistent wines. An unusual speciality is that older vintages can be specially disgorged for customers. The house style is dominated by the full flavours of Pinot Noir.

Pannier
23 rue Roger Catillon, 02403 Château-Thierry. Tel 03 23 69 13 10; fax 03 23 69 18 18. ✓① pp.28, 31
This large co-operative with vast premises on the hill above the town presents a combination of old and new on a single site. In the extensive underground cellars it is necessary to stoop to pass from one to the next, but, in contrast, the wine-making equipment is ultra high-tech. There is a wide range of good to

very good wines: the Cuvée Spéciale Rosé, Louis Eugène, is the top Champagne.

Joseph Perrier
69 avenue de Paris, 51016 Châlons-en-Champagne. Tel 03 26 68 29 51; fax 03 26 70 57 16. ⊘ ① pp.18, 21
One of the few Champagne producers in Châlons, Joseph Perrier now belongs to Laurent-Perrier. Unlike many other leading houses where the style is well established, the wines are less consistent. Generally, they are well rounded and fruity – best is the de luxe Cuvée Josephine.

Perrier-Jouët
26-28 avenue de Champagne, 51200 Épernay. Tel 03 26 55 20 53; fax 03 26 54 54 55. ⊘ ① p.24
The best of the Champagne houses still owned by the Canadian multinational Seagram, Perrier-Jouët makes a reasonable non-vintage, called Grand Brut, but is best known for its rich vintage wine and the de luxe cuvée, Belle Époque, which is famous for its embossed Art Nouveau label.

Cave Vinicole de Pfaffenheim
5 rue du Chai, 68250 Pfaffenheim. Tel 03 89 78 08 88; fax 03 89 49 71 65. ⊘ ● ① ① pp.66, 69
This large Alsace co-operative is also one of the region's best. There is a wide range of wines, including the well-known Hartenberger Crémant d'Alsace. The functional buildings are very well organized for visitors, with tasting facilities and sound advice from a *sommelier*.

Philipponnat
13 rue du Pont, 51160 Mareuil-sur-Ay. Tel 03 26 52 60 43; fax 03 26 52 61 49. ⊘ ① pp.18, 21
This interesting small Champagne house is situated right by the Marne and its canal. On the whole, these are Champagnes of character that require some aging after release. The rare single-vineyard Clos des Goisses can be one of the greatest of Champagnes, powerful and full-bodied.

Pol Roger
1 rue Henri Lelarge, 51220 Épernay. Tel 03 26 59 58 07; fax 03 26 55 25 70. ⊘ ① p.24
Pol Roger is well known as having been Sir Winston Churchill's favourite Champagne and when you step through the firm's door, you enter another age, when being polite and welcoming to visitors was a natural way of life. The top-class wines are among the most delicately balanced of all Champagnes.

Pommery
5 place de Général Gouraud, 51100 Reims. Tel 03 26 61 62 63; fax 03 26 61 63 98. ⊘ ① p.13
Part of the LVMH group, Pommery has splendid buildings, grounds and chalk cellars and is well worth a visit for these alone, although it will also enable you to see one of Reims's rare vineyards. Pommery's is planted with Chardonnay. The style of the wines is generally light and crisp. The prestige cuvée, Louise Pommery, is produced solely from Pommery's top vineyards.

Louis Roederer
21 boulevard Lundy, 51100 Reims. Tel 03 26 40 42 11; fax 03 26 47 66 51. ⊘ ① p.15
Including its various subsidiaries, Roederer is now the largest family-owned Champagne house. Famous above all for its superbly elegant Roederer Cristal, it deserves more recognition for the rest of its range – these are beautifully crafted, sometimes slightly austere and impeccably dosed Champagnes. It is worth getting an introduction and fixing an appointment to visit the magnificent buildings and cellars, which manage to combine the functional and the aesthetic.

Both the surroundings and the Champagnes are full of class, exemplary and very much for connoisseurs.

Rolly Gassmann
2 rue de l'Église, 68590 Rohrschwihr. Tel 03 89 73 63 28; fax 03 89 73 33 06. ⊘ ● ① pp.54, 59
You will receive a splendid Alsatian welcome and generosity here, in a rather dingy cellar but with a huge range of wines that seem to bring the sun flooding in when tasted. The basic range of wines is full of fruit and deliciously drinkable. The top Vendanges Tardives are big and sumptuous. All the wines are made in an exuberant and richly, fruity style that is part of the charm and attraction of Alsace's wines.

Ruinart
4 rue des Crayères, 51100 Reims. Tel 03 26 77 51 51; fax 03 26 82 88 43. ⊘ ① p.13
Founded in 1729, Ruinart is the oldest of the Grande Marque Champagne houses and is now part of the LVMH group. Given the high quality of its wines, it has a surprisingly low profile. The wines are elegant, rather than powerful, and very consistent. The chalk cellars are some of the most spectacular in the *crayères* area of Reims.

Salon
5 rue de la Brèche d'Oger, 51190 le Mesnil-sur-Oger. Tel 03 26 57 51 65; fax 03 26 57 79 29. ⊘ ① pp.37, 39
Salon is one of Champagne's delightful eccentricities. A *négociant* house owned by Laurent-Perrier, it uses only Chardonnay grapes from a single village, le Mesnil, and the wine is released only in top vintages after it has had considerable bottle age. The result is majestic, austere and very concentrated and few other Champagnes can equal it for depth and power. Despite this, it is still a touch less expensive than some other top Champagnes. The elegant winery buildings overlook the vineyards.

Charles Schleret

1–3 route d'Ingersheim, 68230 Turckheim.Tel 03 89 27 06 09. ⊘⊙ p.69
This Alsace grower makes excellent fruity wines and there are particularly good Muscat and Gewurztraminer wines.

Domaines Schlumberger

100 rue Théodore Deck, 68501 Guebwiller. Tel 03 89 74 27 00; fax 03 89 74 85 75. ⊘⊙ pp.67, 69
This is the largest wine estate in Alsace, with 140ha of vineyards. Half of these rate as Grand Cru and are spectacularly steep and terraced. The resulting wines are notably rich and powerful and can be very long-lived. There are excellent Riesling and Gewurztraminer from the Kitterlé Grand Cru and Gewurztraminer Cuvée Christine. Prices tend to be high.

Domaine Schoffit

66–68 Nonnenholzweg, 68000 Colmar. Tel 03 89 24 41 14; fax 03 89 41 40 52. ⊘⊙ pp.59, 67, 69
Situated on the outskirts of Colmar, Robert Schoffit, along with Léonard Humbrecht, is one of the pioneers involved in re-planting the mythical Rangen vineyard at Thann. He makes very aromatic wines in a rounded, almost sweet style. You will receive a friendly welcome along with an informal tasting.

François Secondé

6 rue des Galipes, 51500 Sillery. Tel 03 26 49 16 67; fax 03 26 49 11 55. ⊘⊙⊙ pp.17, 21
The wine village of Sillery, close to Reims, used to be known as one of Champagne's best. This small grower makes very good wines, one of them un-dosed, from a mere 4ha of vines planted with both Pinot Noir and

Chardonnay. He also makes a rare Sillery red which sells under the Coteaux Champenois AC.

Jacques Selosse

22 rue Ernest Vallé, 51190 Avize. Tel 03 26 57 53 56; fax 03 26 57 78 22. ⊘⊙ pp.36, 39
When Anselme Selosse began to use new oak barrels for some of his wines, many people in Champagne threw up their hands in horror. Then he gradually moved into bio-dynamic methods in the vineyard and the same people thought he was just crazy. But anyone who tastes his Champagne has to admit that his idealistic and scrupulous approach has proved many points. The wines are classified according to their nature, rather than conformist conventions. They have great intensity and benefit immensely from extended aging.

F. Servaux Fils

2 rue de Champagne, 02850 Passy-sur-Marne. Tel 03 23 70 35 65; fax 03 23 70 59 99. ⊘⊙ p.28
This grower in the Marne Valley makes well-made, traditional Champagnes at reasonable prices.

De Sousa et Fils

12 place Léon Bourgeois, 51190 Avize. Tel 03 26 57 53 29; fax 03 26 52 30 64. ⊘⊙ pp.37, 39
A small Champagne house run by a young couple, Erick and Michelle de Sousa, who make stylish wines with a softish edge. This makes them easier to drink young than some from this part of the Côte des Blancs.

Alain Soutiran

12 rue St-Vincent, 51150 Ambonnay. Tel 03 26 57 07 87; fax 03 26 57 81 74. ⊘⊙⊙ p.21
The grower, Alain Soutiran, produces some powerful Champagnes, including a Blanc de Blancs not common in this area, from a 15ha vineyard in Ambonnay. Most unusually, he sells other wines together with his own in a cellar wine shop in the village.

Domaine Spielmann

2 route de Thannenkirch, 68750 Bergheim. Tel 03 89 73 35 95; fax 03 89 73 22 49. ⊘⊙ pp.55, 59
When you visit here, you wonder if you've come to the right place, since the house lies behind a builders' merchant. Sylvie Spielmann is a dynamic young woman who makes wines with strong personalities, particularly the Rieslings from the Grand Cru Kanzlerberg.

Taittinger

9 place St-Nicaise, 51100 Reims. Tel 03 26 85 45 35; fax 03 26 85 17 46. ⊘⊙ p.13
Taittinger is one of the few independent Champagne houses and although the main premises are in Reims, its best vineyards are in the Côte des Blancs. Its Champagnes are thus dominated by Chardonnay and are generally light and fresh. The top wine, Comtes de Champagne Blanc de Blancs, is generally superb – finely aromatic creamy Chardonnay at its best. The chalk cellars, in the *crayères* area of Reims, are very impressive and worth visiting.

Tarlant

51480 Oeuilly. Tel 03 26 58 30 60; fax 03 26 58 37 31. ⊘⊙ pp.27, 31
This enterprising family business goes to enormous trouble to reverse the sometimes unwelcoming attitude of Champagne's growers. In this small village, perched on the hillside overlooking the river Marne, Tarlant makes a fairly full-bodied style of Champagne, with a barrel-fermented special blend, called Cuvée Louis Brut. Tarlant runs a bed and breakfast establishment next door.

Emmanuel Tassin

Grande Rue, 10110 Celles-sur-Ource. Tel 03 25 38 59 44; fax 03 25 29 94 59. ⊘⊙ p.44
From a tiny, family-owned vineyard in the Aube which, until recently, sold all its grapes to Champagne houses, Tassin makes an excellent Blanc de Noirs Champagne.

Marc Tempé

16 et 24 rue de Schlossberg, 68340 Zellenberg. Tel & fax 03 89 47 85 22. ⊘ ⓘ pp.56, 59
This young producer used to be an advisor for the national body for French viticulture. In 1995 he started to make his own wine. and very good it is too. His wife runs la Sommelière, Colmar's best wine shop.

Domaine F E Trimbach

15 route de Bergheim, 68150 Ribeauvillé. Tel 03 89 73 60 30; fax 03 89 73 89 04. ⊘ ⓘ pp.55, 59
This excellent *négociant* makes very reliable wines at all prices and also owns some top-quality vineyards. The most famous is the Clos Ste-Hune at Hunawihr and the Riesling from here is one of Alsace's truly great wines. The Trimbach style of Riesling is dry, subtly perfumed and well balanced throughout and the reserve Cuvée Frédéric-Émile is another excellent wine. Trimbach's curious tower makes its location easy to spot in the village. The tasting takes place in a spacious shop on the same site.

Cave Vinicole de Turckheim

16 rue de Tuileries, 68230 Turckheim. Tel 03 89 27 06 25; fax 03 89 27 35 33. ⊘ ⓘ ⓘ ⓘ p.69
This is one of the best and most reliable of Alsace's wine co-operatives, with more than 250 members. It makes mainly white wine and has a particularly good reputation for excellent Pinot Blanc and Tokay-Pinot Gris, as well as good Gewurztraminer and Crémant d'Alsace. There is a little deliciously fruity Pinot Noir and fine rosé.

De Venoge

30 avenue de Champagne, 51200 Épernay. Tel 03 26 53 34 46; fax 03 26 53 34 35. ⊘ ⓘ p.24
Based in elegant buildings in the heart of Épernay's Champagne quarter, this house is now part of the Rémy-Martin group and has a good stock of well-aged Champagnes with a rich and toasty character. There is also an unusual vintage Blanc de Noirs.

Jean Vesselle

4 rue Victor-Hugo, 51150 Bouzy. Tel 03 26 57 01 55; fax 03 26 57 06 95. ⊘ ⓘ ⓘ pp.18, 21
There are many members of the Vesselle family in Bouzy but Jean Vesselle is perhaps the most reliable, in terms of the quality of his wines. Red Bouzy Rouge complements some lightly dosed Champagnes.

Veuve Clicquot Ponsardin

1 place des Droits de l'Homme, 51100 Reims. Tel 03 26 89 54 40; fax 03 26 40 60 17. ⊘ ⓘ p.13
These Champagnes can still live up to the high standards set by the Veuve or Widow Clicquot who invented the *remuage* system in the early 19th century. Now one of the largest producers, at around 10 million bottles a year, it also manages to be one of the most reliable for its Brut non-vintage. There is an excellent range of wines, which tend to benefit from some cellar aging.

Vve A Devaux

Domaine de Villeneuve, 10110 Bar-sur-Seine. Tel 03 25 38 30 65; fax 03 25 29 73 21. ⊘ ⓘ ⓘ p.45
This is a brand name used by the Union Auboise, the largest co-operative in the Aube region. The Champagnes are made in a modern, fresh style. There is also very good Rosé des Riceys.

Champagne Vilmart

4 rue de la République, 51500 Rilly-la-Montagne. Tel 03 26 03 40 01; fax 03 26 03 46 57. ⊘ ⓘ p.21
This long-established Champagne house is also able to draw upon its own 11ha of Premier Cru vineyards. Using traditional wine-making (both the fermentation and aging take place in oak barrels), the wines

include a light, delicate non-vintage, called Grand Cellier, a refined vintage, Grand Cellier d'Or, and a sumptuous Coeur de Cuvée.

Bernard Weber

49 route de Saverne, 67120 Molsheim. Tel 03 88 38 52 67; fax 03 88 38 58 81. ⊘ ⓘ pp.52, 59
This small Alsace grower makes excellent wines, mostly in a dry style. There are also some fine Vendanges Tardives, produced only in the ripest years.

Domaine Weinbach

Clos des Capucins, 68240 Kaysersberg. Tel 03 89 47 13 21; fax 03 89 47 38 18. ⊘ ⓘ pp.62, 69
The estate is now run by Mme Faller and her daughters, who continue the tradition of bottling and selling each cask of wine separately. The top wine is the Riesling Cuvée Ste-Cathérine but all the wines are good, from the simple Pinot Blanc and Sylvaner to the sumptuous Gewurztraminer Vendanges Tardives and Sélections de Grains Nobles. Tasting here is a memorable experience.

Zind-Humbrecht

4 route de Colmar, 68230 Turckheim. Tel 03 89 27 02 05; fax 03 89 27 22 58. ⊘ ⓘ pp.64, 67, 69
This is undisputedly one of the star estates in Alsace. The Humbrechts, father and son, pursue a rigorous approach to terroir and wine-making to produce some of Alsace's most powerfully structured and aromatic wines. They own vines in 4 Grands Crus (Rangen, Goldert, Hengst and Brand) and these wines (Riesling, Pinot Gris, Gewurztraminer and Muscat) are excellent, as are their Vendanges Tardives. It is hard to find an uninspiring wine but some are not for the weak hearted, and they are also among the hardest to acquire, thanks to worldwide demand. The new building is architecturally daring, but functional.

Index of Wine Villages and Other Wine Producers

Picture Credits
Principal photographer Mick Rock (Cephas Picture Library); other Cephas photographers: Herve Amiard 11; Ikko Blythe 29; Nigel Blythe 17; Christine Fleurent 10; M J Kielty 52, 59; Jarry Tripelon 49, 54. Other photographs supplied by Michael Busselle 31, 43; Janet Price 26, 53.
Publisher's Acknowledgments Trevor Lawrence (map illustrations), Aziz Khan (grape artworks), Steven Marwood (bottle photography).